America's
Real Deficit

*Is Character Disorder
Everywhere?*

JOE COUCH, MBA

ISBN: 1463744692

ISBN-13: 978-1463744694

**This book is dedicated
to
the future of America**

CONTENTS

Preface   1

1 How to Read Math   2

2 The Return on   13
   Higher Education

3 Stories of Work life   26

4 Healthcare   54

5 Compensation and   71
   Philanthropy

6 The Americans with   91
   Disability Act

7 The Leadership Deficit   127
   in Not-For-Profits

8 Conclusion   134

9 About the Author   136

PREFACE

In an earlier book I went into depth about cognitive dissonance, voids in character, and their influence on America's political and economic issues ("*Polarization in America!*" (*PIA*)). For those seeking more of the PIA flavor, you'll find the same underlying theory about American apathy is maintained, but I alert you that this book differs in tone, as we're going into some cesspool issues of American life as an endeavor to elevate the dialogue.

While I am committed to an inquiring perspective, I have reached some settled opinions through research, interviews, and personal experience about some of the topics covered. I endeavor to call these perspectives out, tell you where my bias is and why.

I understand that some may feel a bit picked on, but the sectors chosen to be highlighted in this book were selected because I am optimistic that we can have a less dysfunctional America in the future; however, to get there, I believe some serious issues need to be aired, and hopefully, laundered.

So - let's get down to business.

HOW TO READ MATH

I believe that the media and the political parties somewhat consciously manipulate to enhance political and economic polarization in this country, polarization that generally benefits a relatively small number of people. They are able to do this because we as individuals have let them, but I also contend that we have not really prepared our citizens for the complexity of adulthood, for skills that are needed to think in an integrated way so that we can better evaluate the polarizing messages that come our way.

Education is the first step towards a more complete discussion about adult life. I contend that America's future depends on a populace that is educated about *the core issues that matter*, and that a good place to start would be to teach financial literacy in high schools.

BOOMER MATH

I am starting this chapter out perhaps not exactly where you thought it would start: with Baby Boomers, and I do so because many of them seem not to have been taught how to do life's math.

On the positive side, Baby Boomers, born after 1946 through 1964, were the first group to genuinely assume that the world would improve. Notably, they worked to break down the confines of traditional roles, roles which arguably bound people to limited experiences of life (Jones, Landon (1980), *Great Expectations: America and the Baby Boom Generation).*

And with their numbers, *"Baby Boomers control over 80% of personal financial assets and more than 50% of discretionary spending power... They are responsible for more than half of all consumer spending, buy 77% of all prescription drugs, 61% of OTC medication and 80% of all leisure travel..."* (Wikipedia).

In sum, Baby Boomers served as the impetus for, and continue the drive of, the consumer society. They created demands for credit. They got cheap education when education was cheap and they did not have to buy insurance for every little thing when they were young and trying to save money. Most of them will likely get most, if not all, of their expected Social Security payments.

They are the first "me first" group and they passed those "*me first*" attitudes to their children and other younger people. Some were able to buy houses low, sell them high, and move out of the expensive areas, netting huge amounts of cash by selling price inflated houses to Generation X.

But a lot of the Boomers, because either they were too cocky in the stock market or they bought too much stuff instead of saving their money, now feel that they face an economically uncertain future. A lot of them freaked out, took out what cash they had left at the bottom of the stock market drop to preserve it and so did not recoup their losses when the stock market recovered.

The result: a good number of the older ones are not quitting their jobs as expected at 65, 68, even 70. In my opinion, these ones probably did not know how to do math, or live too large, or did not save enough, or admittedly, perhaps they just like to make money and stay busy. So a lot of them are now double dipping with salary and Social Security (or triple dipping if they have a pension as well).

Guess what that is doing? Younger people who would normally be promoted into higher responsibility jobs are unemployed or underemployed. It's not enough to suggest this is somehow *unfair*. And why it's not enough to suggest that it is simply *unfair* is that it is also going to create a leadership problem in 7 to 15 years, when we would expect people in their early 50's to take on crucial senior roles that require 15 to 20 years of managerial experience.

I have concerns that America will get worse should it have to rely on a cadre of less experienced managers in business, education, and government. In other words, Boomers' desire to "stay busy", should they not need the money, is potentially harming America's future leadership pool.

My opinion: if they can afford it, Boomers should go be unpaid volunteers somewhere and open up these opportunities. And some do volunteer, to SCORE for instance, but I am talking about the ones who have not left the workforce, and the impact of that trend on our future.

But what we also see in the Boomers, and not to assign blame to them in total for this scenario, for it took a lot of generations to get here, but they are the first group where the toxicity of voids in character took hold.

Veterans perhaps aside, Boomers pushed for a free-wheeling society and basically institutionalized the idea of *"what's in it for me?".* And thus, at minimum, they helped make exponential the problems we face.

In my opinion, the only reason to feel sorry for the best off (on average) group that will probably ever live on this planet is this: their high schools probably did not teach them basic finance and many of them may thus be in dire situations later.

We should be very worried that currently schools do not teach it, but with the Boomers, we can see some proof of how this omission has impacted America, and if nothing else, that's the lesson we should be paying more attention to.

BUT IT DOES NOT PAY
TO TEACH FINANCE TO KIDS

To address the issue, first I want to make a point: it is not *home ownership* until you have the house or condo paid off, it is *mortgage ownership,* and we see that a mortgage is a large thing to own: from

Interest.com, the average 30 year mortgage, if all payments are made, is comprised of about 50% interest and 50% principal.

On a $500,000 mortgage for a 30 year loan at 5%, the interest payments are about $466,000, for a total in payments of $966,000. That means the cash out of pocket, when fully paid off, is about twice the price if the buyer takes 30 years to pay it off.

If you learn the math of this in high school, when your brain is still freshly going "*What the ....?"* to just about every dumb thing you see going on in adulthood, then you probably would not want to buy a house until you had a big cash down payment or you could afford the higher payments on a 15 year mortgage, which cuts interest payments by over half.

That means you probably would not be spending money on a 60" TV at age 22, you would be *saving* it.

And so who does not want people to save money and so why is finance not taught to America's high school kids?

Keeping it real: in America, just about every special interest group, including the government would rather people spend than save, which provides little to no incentive to insist on finance education in the high schools.

Why? Because you would be taught to **save** more of the money they would prefer you spend on stuff.

So why some people might encourage long mortgages is so that monthly payments are low enough such that you still have enough left to buy stuff, consumer products, which due to materials and by design, are going to break or otherwise not be useful within about 3 years.

This expected 3 year product cycle often requires people to replace stuff. For instance, certain items like computers have a 3 year depreciation timeline when you are talking taxes. That means that one way a company can deduct the expense of a 3 year item is to divide its cost by three and deduct it equally over the 3 years - that's called "straight line depreciation".

The useful length of life for a product is matched to the tax deduction a business can take for it. As such, there is a big incentive for computer fabricators to create new software or new hardware to last give or take, you can guess: 3 years, because then businesses can start on a new deduction cycle.

Is it wrong to plan on 3 year breakage? I do not think so, because things break due to materials wear anyway. But, just because they come up with a new version does not mean you have to buy it if there's really nothing wrong with the one you have - and *not buying every new thing is how a lot of people save money*, and that's my point, and just about everyone would learn it if they taught financial know-how in high school.

Another interesting thing that happens with a long mortgage is high interest rates are paid on the loan, which create valuable income for people like me. Mortgage bond interest is income that pensions and other investors receive to hold the bonds. In a diversified retirement account, many people have 20 to 30% of their bonds in "mortgage backed" bonds.

Those relatively large payments have come to be depended upon by pension plans, retirees, and Wall Street bond houses (who strip and flip the standard mortgage into several types of seductive and risky gambling-type options). The bonds pay more in interest if the mortgage owner does not: 1) put a whole lot down as a down payment, and 2) takes 30 years to pay it off.

So, the investors would probably freak out a bit if all of a sudden people bought houses with 50 to 100% down in cash. They would not have as many interest-lush bonds available to buy, it would cause bidding up of the prices, and they generally do not want that: thus they have no incentive to support teaching high school students finance.

Also, government, at many levels, wants you to be a spender for tax reasons. It simply does not bring as much revenue to the government if Americans save significantly more and not buy things that trigger sales tax, use tax, or income tax.

And, while it seems the Federal government should have little reason to prefer one form of taxation over another, the fact is that they have structured the tax system so that, for most people, the interest income from those mortgage bonds is taxed at a *higher* rate than the dividends or gains that come from stocks.

Think they want interest income from long term mortgages to go away?

Think they want young people to understand what I am saying?

You decide.

COGNITIVE DISSONANCE
AND DEFINITION OF CHARACTER

So, to sum it up, business wants Americans to have surplus money to spend on stuff, and, because other people want a piece of the mortgage interest pie, there is no incentive for anyone to teach high school students what they really maybe, probably, should know about finance.

As a point of self-disclosure, I find myself in some mental conflict (or *cognitive dissonance*) about bonds: I find have some anxiety with the idea that there might not be plenty of interest-rich mortgages available to invest in, since I have some retirement funds with those bonds in them.

My question: *Would we be able to pay less in taxes in the **future** if I were willing to give up some interest points on my mortgage bonds **now**?*

9

My mental conflict about mortgages has completely to do with what I do not want to give up: future retirement income, and so my personal tendency is *denial*, to tell myself things really won't be that bad in the future.

And if high mortgage bond interest all went away I'd probably feel the pinch; still, I have to ask myself if we would have a different country were teenagers educated about finance. I can't help but think that our nation's debt would be lower, probably Social Security would be more secure and maybe my Top Ten problems list might be only a Top Six list.

But what is all this about mental conflict or ***cognitive dissonance****, you might ask?*

From Wikipedia, ***cognitive dissonance*** is defined as

*"... **an uncomfortable feeling caused by holding conflicting ideas simultaneously. The theory of cognitive dissonance proposes that people have a motivational drive to reduce dissonance. They do this by changing their attitudes, beliefs, and actions. Dissonance is also reduced by justifying, blaming, and denying.**"*

I contend that how people respond to their cognitive dissonance is *why* we have so many problems in America today; it should suffice to say that I contend that we resolve our dissonance or mental conflict in ways that allow ***voids in character*** to persist and reproduce, since many Americans regularly ignore or minimize the impact that the bad behavior of others has on us.

And not to pitch any particular definition of character, but I think it would be helpful to at least give one idea of how the definition of character can be framed - feel free to add or subtract a trait or two to suit your own purposes.

Wikipedia describes the concept of character as

"*a variety of attributes including the existence   or lack of virtues such as integrity, courage, fortitude, honesty, and loyalty...*".

In a nut shell, what I mean by *void in character* is that at least one or more of these core behavioral expectations are *lacking or totally nonexistent* in the person's behavior or in an event under discussion; and along with cognitive dissonance, that's what this book's all about -- and together, they are why finance is not taught: the impact of doing it is mentally conflicting for those who make those decisions.

NEO-CONSERVATIVE IS NOT A DIRTY WORD NOW THAT I HAVE MONEY

To close out this chapter, I feel it behooves me to mention that I believe the Left, people who claim to want greater class parity, have failed to live up to their ideals in the education of the young. They are simply not doing one of the most important things they could insist upon for greater class parity: the financial education of youth.

I guess when trying to sort out why *doing nothing* has been their approach, I feel we might not have to go far. It's perhaps really no surprise that the playwright David Mamet "converted" away from liberalism, denouncing it heavily in his book "*The Secret Knowledge: On the Dismantling of American Culture*". Why is it no surprise?

Well, now he has assets, and lots of them.

It's been my observation that once those on the Left have increased assets and receive inheritances, they become almost neo-conservatives, at least economically. I believe we will see a continued shift as wealthy Left-leaning Boomers *use every vehicle possible* to avoid taxes, just like the wealthy on the Right have done for generations.

These instruments include what are called "bypass trusts", designed to help descendants avoid paying high estate taxes. Well, income tax and estate tax are just shades of the same cloth, and in my opinion, it's **hypocrisy** to use the same legal techniques the Right has used to avoid paying taxes and **then** politically contend that it is *wrong* for the rich to get richer. In other words, some of them have become the "*them*" whom they criticize.

Ahhh, how it pays to keep the young ignorant and just maybe: "*the Left **is** the new Right*".

THE RETURN ON
HIGHER EDUCATION

In our next step towards an expanded discussion of character, it's important to take a brief look at college education. In my opinion, some people should never go to college. I believe more high schools should have technical and vocational tracks for those uninterested in the dry cerebral tasks required to complete a four to five year degree. Some people's gifts lie elsewhere.

A master level BMW mechanic makes about $120K, and midrange, they make about $70K, and we need people to be able to fix those and other cars. But are sufficient numbers of students told of these opportunities in high school so they can make appropriate decisions?

No, the social message is that people should buckle under, go to a four year college and that choosing *anything less is just not acceptable*, or so the millions spent to market college education tells us. But the belief system that many have adopted about educational status may be causing too much pressure and debt to make it worthwhile for all.

I read recently about a guy who caught Derek Jeter's 3,000th baseball hit. The fellow gave the ball back to Jeter instead of putting it up for auction. Some said "stupid move", and perhaps maybe it really was not so bright since the guy has *over a hundred thousand dollars* in college debt, and at the time of the catch, he was working as a cell phone salesman.

So, how are his loans going to be paid off? It will probably take the guy's entire life, and school loans now follow people through bankruptcy, so there is no out there. They say he'd likely have secured 6 figures for the ball if he auctioned it off. Maybe if he had finance in high school, he would have kept the ball.

But here's my question: *would this guy have been better off in a two year technical college?* Could be.

See, what if Junior does not want to be a lawyer?

Isn't being a human resources specialist a decent job? It might be good enough for him or for her, especially if that means they get to be with their kids more often *and* they are debt free in 5 years.

THE MBA AS AN EXAMPLE OF MARKETING

This book does not exist to whine about my life, and I won't since I don't really have much to whine about as compared with most Americans, but perhaps what I have to say about getting an MBA is true about a lot of other degrees too.

First, all of the MBA programs in America have to use **the same** curriculum or they are not able to be accredited. What does that mean? That means the first year at almost every MBA program covers the same material, often using the same textbooks. Also, most schools use the *Harvard Business Review Cases,* a set of hypothetical or fictionalized cases presented to students in the format of basically,

"What would you do if this happened and why?"

The business cases are used in the second year too, often heavily, and while that helps ensure employers of a certain level of shared knowledge, it also shows there are not many differences in what's learned by students.

And so you ask:

"So, Joe, what's all this about rankings then?"

In my opinion, it's pretty much baloney. The ranks are about what groupiness you want to *pay* for - do you want the groupiness of Wharton, UCLA, or Yale - or - is staying local more important to getting a job? The schools pitch the idea that if you go to a higher ranked one, you'll be able to pay off the $100K faster than a horse can spit across a river. All told, because it was some years ago, I took out about $35,000 and it's paid off, but not as fast as I thought it would be based on projections presented by the lender.

My point: The ranks are all pretty much marketing manipulation targeted to our emotions about what we think we need to achieve the American Dream. That said, I can't say that grad school did not help me, because the MBA degree has, but I am not sure how much the specific school I went to did. I think a good regional school is fine, and I know of plenty of

C-level folks who did not go to a nationally ranked school. It's what you do with it.

But another point I want to make is that there is now a much stronger emphasis on ranks than there used to be even 10 years ago. I think it is helping promote the fiction that a high ranked degree is the only way to become successful.

Schools have hired large numbers of marketing staff over the last 20 years where there once were few to none. Back in the day, colleges might have had a small PR department, but now colleges are in lock step with corporations, with marketing specialists and publicity teams dedicated to raising the school's rank; somehow, it's supposed to help make you feel more confident that it is money well spent.

Here's the rub: I did not need to go to college, let alone get a ranked MBA, to have confidence, and my point is, neither do a lot of other people - as long as they have financial literacy, as long as they find training appropriate to what they are drawn to do, and as long as their jobs are not exported out of the country in ways that perhaps make no sense.

As Jesse James said in one of his motorcycle shows, to paraphrase, people should not be ashamed that they are good with their hands. And as Cher said in an interview some years ago, and I paraphrase, the bus driver should be proud to be a bus driver and the rest of us should treat the bus driver with more respect.

It takes all kinds to create a village, and in the archetype of earlier times, our minds often have a clear picture of a small town, perhaps helped by Richard Scarry books, but nonetheless we picture: a butcher, a baker, a candlestick maker, a school bus driver, a policeman, a mayor, a thief, an attorney, a preschool teacher, a minister, an artist, a musician, the barkeep, and so forth.

It is a social fabric of what our minds expect life to be - with complexity and diversity, with a range of educational accomplishment and with a range of economic classes, living mostly in harmony and an acceptance of difference.

So, why do we now seem to ignore the community value in all of these roles and want everyone to be a doctor or a lawyer or a rock star? Has the media really been able to sell a high bill of goods as the only valued way to live a life?

My questions:

Is the rise in dissatisfaction within America due to people not having food on the table or is it because they do not feel they have enough stuff to prove they've "made it"?

Does not having "enough" induce people to rationalize behaving badly in order to get what they think they deserve?

WHY A PH.D. IS OFTEN NOW A "F.U.D."

As in, that's an "Eff'ing Useless Degree"!

(Excuse my *french*, but in this case, it's *appropos*)

So let's take a look at universities today. In sum, it's my opinion that some have been bought and paid for by intellectual property-seeking corporate interests and by endowment patrons seeking to marquee their family name across buildings. I believe most people "in the know" believe that MIT is now basically a lab for professors developing patents, supported by corporate interests.

Is that a bad thing by itself?

Maybe not. I am not sure. I am *just saying*. My point is that it's good to be educated about this stuff and understand how things are inter-related. People and institutions often have motives that are not transparent, and if you do not know that universities are now highly profit motivated in much the same way businesses are, then you are missing a big piece of why things happen the way they do.

It's in this context that we now find that it is often the case that graduate students in Ph.D. programs are treated like indentured servants, all seeking the golden nectar of, I would say *knowledge*, but really, many are there for the *prestige* of a Ph.D.. A friend of a friend openly admitted at a cocktail party that the reason for his seeking a Ph.D. soon is "*for his ego*".

And so I will say it: I believe we are using the Federal grant system to fund the *prestige* building efforts of individuals when we simply no longer need people to become that well trained for the jobs that now exist.

No, you might say, *it's to continue an investment in knowledge we need for America's future.* No, I stifle a small laugh, as the *Nature* recently explained ("*Education: The PhD factory*", April 20, 2011).

Noting the work of Paula Stephan at Georgia State, the article stated there are few tenure tracks available and that we are now training too many Ph.D.'s, especially in the sciences. We're pushing out about 20,000 a year, but industry has few jobs for them. We are oversaturated and will be for a long while.

Is it time to put the F.U.D. factories on hold?

You decide.

Why are there no places in academia? Well, the old (and I mean *old* - like 75 - 80 year old) professors are sticking around until they and their battery powered scooters run out of charge.

Maybe *these* are the guys who live too large or buy too many tech stocks. Perhaps they have convinced themselves that they *need* the money, so they rationalize staying on well past their prime, even though many of them are already pensioners, double or triple dipping for income; and that rationalization only occurs if any *cognitive dissonance* shows its head.

I feel I can probably assure you, should some older professors ever stop to wonder if they might be preventing the younger generation's development of teaching and research skills, that they likely do not care. I highly doubt that many of them care that a lack of developed leadership in universities may have a lasting impact on this nation.

They are too busy lobbying in Washington for that $4 million to study the mating habits of sterilized rats (note: *this grant example made up to protect the potentially guilty*). That and it's well known that professors are generally pro's at "*what's in it for me?*"

Ahhh, the *publish or perish* ego!

WHAT A "FRESH HEAD" CAN DO

So why are there so many openings in Ph.D. programs if we do not have the demand for labor **after** they graduate? Maybe it's because the universities "need" the fresh cheap labor **before** they graduate to teach courses so the professors do not have to.

In other words, the math shows that the Federal government (yes, us through taxes and by being willing to increase the debt ceiling annually) awards research grants that are used to subsidize salaries of cheap teaching labor. For most traditional Ph.D. students, probably about 20,000 of them per year, the grant and the school each pay part of their income.

The Nature article did not say it per se, but this Joe has the dots close enough together now to suggest that this conclusion is just so: and it's why we have too many people with F.U.D.'s.

Shouldn't something about this change?

You decide.

If the schools filled half the teaching spots with a Master's degree level person, at a decent wage with benefits, I believe that about 10,000 spots for new Ph.D. students would drop because they would no longer be needed; the market would come back to a closer balance.

Admittedly, by doing so, it would likely be another excuse for universities to raise fees in order to pay a living wage to the Master's degree instructors, but *our* Federal debt would likely drop because *they* would stop funding *optional* research programs.

I am not saying that some of the grants are not justified *if the country has surplus funds*, but these days we need to tighten the belt. Perhaps what should matter to us is that if a Federal grant is large enough, people come out of Ph.D. programs with little to no debt - should they not pay something? That friend of a friend expects to owe less than $50,000 once done. Moreover, he admitted that he will receive *no additional salary once he is done with the Ph.D. than he gets now* - again, his Ph.D. is for *prestige*.

Compare that with the fellow who caught Jeter's 3,000[th] ball. Our economy probably needs the ball-catcher's degree sooner than F.U.D. person's degree, and yet who owes/will owe more?

And while Ph.D. not only gets away without much debt at all, we the taxpayer are expected to take on *more* Federal debt through the awarding of *more* Federal grants that were the only reason why Ph.D. guy will not incur much debt. And now, according to *Nature*, we find out this training is unneeded.

But, as Future-F.U.D. gleamed over his 3rd martini, he's going to have *fun* for 4 years because he "*hates corporate America*". He just found out the grant was approved, so he is in like Flynn. Lucky us, we get to pay for his prestige, regardless if he adds any real economic value to our country.

My questions:

- *Doesn't this situation make American universities basically another special interest group?*

- *Aren't the professors really paid lobbyists when they visit D.C. since they are seeking to direct legislation driven dollars to their university?*

- *Shouldn't they be required to register as lobbyists?*

You decide.

HOW MUCH?!?

Now, I know I could get one of those spanking Ph.D. diplomas and obtain more prestige than I already have. I've looked at some programs, but I've been told it would cost $60-90K just in tuition since they won't offer credit for my two existing years of graduate school and since I would not want one from a major university because they only offer F.U.D. options, at least for me.

Again, they want - no, they require - 3 to 4 years of residency tuition. Why? Well, they now have to pay for the marketing department, you see, to "*attract*" candidates. Now, according to that logic, I would not ever look them up as a possible school to attend unless they had a marketing outreach effort to attract me. Really? *Really*?

It just costs too much. According to the CNN Money website, as of 2011, the College Board stated that tuition and fees increased about 130% over the last 20 years. I read somewhere that a University of California professor, tired of instructional employees being blamed for skyrocketing costs, put a chart on his office door showing that while instructional costs were about flat, administrative costs increased 200% in 10 years; think maybe I have a clue?

So, even though I feel I could get something from it, these schools just want too much of my hard earned net worth, and I have concluded that I don't want one that badly... *but* this research led me to believe that:

EDUCATION IS NOW "BUY-A-DEGREE"

*For sale now! Just $215,000 for a B.S.
from Emory University! Get yours today!*

Are you sticker shocked? I was. But go ahead, get a Political Science degree, party until you drop, and dang, just maybe you will get a spot as a Democratic intern so you can learn how to polarize American politics just like your heroes have been doing for decades. You might even meet Bill Clinton!

I say: *it's ridiculous.*

Our problems are just too large for the shifting of middle-upper class assets to universities to persist indefinitely <u>without</u> a serious price correction, or so you'd think.

What is true is that graduates won't be able to use that supposed private school prestige if they are stuck in a soup kitchen line at age 40 because their parents' Boomer friends refuse to retire from jobs as policy analysts well past normal retirement age.

In my opinion, universities are capitalizing on the fact that the U.S. Census data shows that a bachelor's degree is the door that opens to significantly higher wages. So they are doing what all other ***businesses*** do when they know demand is higher than supply and there is no other option: they raise prices.

And they have raised them a lot, and by doing so, they have proved they understand the situation for what it is, and what any Joe would think: *they are selling bachelor degrees as if they were Bentleys.*

What's sad, or bad, or poses a problem is that there is no competition here to provide downward price pressure: it seems they may have a monopoly. As such, one might think perhaps some oversight body could ask if there is any price fixing going on, something that often happens in *cartels*.

Cartels? Yeah, look it up, see what you think. Does it apply to universities?

You decide.

And what happens these days when graduates have debt, whether from on-line BA programs or from the most prestigious Ph.D. program? Well, a lot of them move back home with the folks.

Some are fortunate to quickly obtain jobs to begin to pay it down, but when they get to work, boy, can they be in for a shock. And so we go - - to peer into what adult work life is often really like.

STORIES OF WORKLIFE

*All of the stories in this book are composites based on one or more stories told to me by others, stories I've read or synthesized from my own experiences, and all have been **fictionalized**. Stories were presented to me as "true from somewhere" but all names, as far as I know, are not those of the people that they may partially represent. No one should conclude that any one person described here refers to any specific person they know.*

I contend that work is where people become inured to bad behavior in our society. If they don't have the pattern in them already, young people are socialized during the first few years in the work world. Often, if - or once - young people experience toxic work environments first hand, they go to parents for advice, and the folks, wanting to protect them, tell them:

- *it's not your problem*

- *stay out of it*

- *do what's best for you*

- *there's no one there protecting you,
  so keep your mouth shut*

While parents, friends, and relatives may have the best interests of these young people at heart, the results of this emphasis on only protecting our own hides has a not so hidden but growing consequence to America as a whole.

For example, this Joe is sick and tired of seeing the careers of some very talented people harmed by the void in character, *"what's in it for me?"* behaviors of a surprisingly large number of dysfunctional others, whose behavior goes on without much consequence because co-workers look the other way or lie to "*do what's best for them*".

And so I offer these vignettes, so you can see exactly what I mean.

STORY 1: *ARE YOU KIDDING?*
I'M NOT HERE FOR THE *CLIENTS*

I think the day I realized that things were irretrievably messed up must have been the day when one of my executive peers, whom I had repeatedly seen writing a fiction novel on her computer during business hours, told me that she thought I should figure out how the agency could pay for her to go to law school within my department's budget.

I asked which of the clients would benefit. She said, "*None, I just want to get a law degree so that when I retire from here, I have something to do.*" and smiled.

In shock, I let it go, and then visited her a few days later and told her it could not be done. She said, "*Are you sure?*" I said *"Yes, I'm sure".* She came by one more time, requesting the same thing, and then when I told her it could not be done again, she asked "*Are you sure?*" I told her I was 100% positive and so she dropped it.

But yeah, I think that was the moment when I took it home that many employees in Not-For-Profits really are there only for "*what's in it for them*".

Later, this particular organization proved that many of them are there only for the money, but probably nothing more arrogantly stands out than this masters-degree'd gal, trying to figure out how she could suck even more wealth out of the organization at the expense of the less fortunate. Her fully loaded compensation package was well over $120,000 per year, so it was not as though she could not pay for it herself.

What was even more shocking was that she was clearly already a millionaire: she drove a luxury car, her husband drove a Ferrari *and* a Hummer, and they owned a vacation home in the mountains, a house boat, and rental properties. In my view, one can have no argument about her success by itself were she not also trying to drink improperly from the agency trough, but it made me wonder how ethical she had been in how she reached success.

And what about those less fortunate people for whom we'd been brought together to serve?

Well, in my opinion, she had little concern for them, for if she had, I would never have been asked to figure out how we could illicitly pay for her law school tuition for three years, a $50-100K+ expense.

And beyond the obvious selfishness and greed, what perhaps should bother you about this?

Last I heard . . . *she's still there*.

STORY 2:   THE SOFTWARE BLUNDER

June had been hired at a large software corporation in their marketing department. Her job was to help with product roll outs, more specifically, to track product launches. The project had been launched several years prior with great fanfare, spearheaded by a rising Vice President. The project had been delayed since that auspicious start: shelved twice and the VP had been shelved as well through layoff.

The project was finally elevated to a strategically important initiative and re-assigned to the team June had joined. Steven and Brenda were the co-leads, one manager each from Marketing and IT. There were 8 people from IT and 4 people total from Marketing, making for a dozen, including the Project Managers.

Steven and Brenda had been given a roll out deadline of 15 months when it was first re-assigned, and the team's project bonuses were tied to the deadline. Everything was going fine, but then the CEO decided to fast track the project, and pushed everything into a new 12 month deadline, against the recommendations of the Project Control Team, or that's what the scuttlebutt had been.

What the CEO did *not* mention to them was that if he cut costs by not paying out bonus money, his stock awards would be increased by 20%, and so he carried a hidden incentive for the team to fail.

The team was now under an impossible deadline. The initial roll out was scheduled for 200 beta customers, rolled to an additional 5,000 customers within the following 12 months. As the deadline loomed, both Steven and Brenda took out their frustration on staff, the IT team members in particular. With 3 months left, the team was wrought with high levels of anxiety, as they felt sure that they could not hit the goal.

Then, rather suddenly, after a weekend working in the office, the IT team joined the weekly meeting and told everyone that everything was now under control, as they had reached a major milestone sooner than expected. In fact, they would finish early. Relief and a sense of joy filled the room. In the following month, the test screening showed a program that seemed to operate well when connected to the company's server. Everyone breathed another sigh of relief:

they would get their bonuses.

So, the IT folks sent the upgrade to the beta customers one week ahead of schedule. A party was had, the champagne poured, even the CEO came down to join in the celebration for about 5 minutes, showering praise on the whole team: *he knew it had been a hard project, but he knew **his** team would muscle through!* They all got the full amount possible for their bonuses. It seemed a happy time for all.

It was June's job to follow up and see how customers were enjoying the functionality of the new upgrade. She sent out an email survey asking for feedback and received 18 replies out of the 200 in the beta group.

Now all the beta customers had specifically agreed to provide feedback as part of gaining early access to the breakthrough upgrade, so a 9% response rate was not expected or acceptable. The company felt that a 75% response rate was the minimum needed to identify broad problems.

However, the responses that came back, as June put it to me, "*were really odd*". She had asked "*Does the new feature do X properly*?" The answer repeatedly was "*No*". This did not seem correct, as June herself had observed the program working during the IT team's demo. June was confused.

She had never seen such a reaction to this type of upgrade. June called some of the customers who had responded and one of them finally told her that the reason the answer to her question was "*No*" was that *he could not get the program to work **at all***.

Dismayed, June took the results to Steven, the Marketing Manager, and he too was confused. He told June he would speak with Brenda about it to see if she had any insight. The next day Steven called June into his office.

He looked slightly embarrassed and told June that the Brenda and the most senior member of the IT team admitted that they had decided it would not hurt to roll out a buggy version to hit the deadline, justified on the basis that they felt the CEO had *set them up for failure* in taking away the 3 months.

Steven also shared that he and Brenda felt the CEO had tried to raid their bonuses by moving the due date. He also told her the reason she did not hear from the other customers was probably because IT admitted that they had sent the upgrade out to *only 20* customers, and so the other customers probably felt her email was in error and ignored it.

Several team meetings were subsequently held to discuss the buggy upgrade and it was also covered in general staff meetings, but Brenda held her ground and said that they had indeed met the deadline, and sure there were a few bugs in the program, but heck, that happens all the time:

"Just look at Microsoft!"

At the end of the debate that wasn't, the CEO decided he did not want anyone really digging into his motives, so they were all able to keep their bonuses, splitting over $100,000, most of it going to Brenda and Steven.

The software was still not functional 6 months after the deadline, and June said it was comical to watch the IT manager wiggle out an explanation month after month. Finally, June realized this was *business as usual* at the company when the same pattern occurred on another project.

June was fortunate, as she was able to quickly find another job in a firm where vaporware and voids in character were not tolerated. There was no one for June to go to about this pattern even had she wished to; it was just the corporate culture of this place.

But I ask you:

- *Even if the CEO was exhibiting voids in character, did not the IT team essentially commit corporate theft of the bonus pool?*

And how do you think they rationalize behavior?

- *Because the CEO did it to us, we are justified in using the same tactics.*

- *Because Microsoft supposedly rolls out buggy software, we can do it too.*

To tie it more broadly: why do politicians perhaps think they can get away with character deficient behavior? Perhaps it's because a good number of voters *are doing it too.*

At least some Americans tell themselves that the bits of bad done by politicians are not that bad, heck, they would do it too if in their shoes.

Further, I believe that too many people think the politician's biggest problem was: "*he got caught*".

STORY 3:   THE WEB DESIGNER

Cheryl had worked her way up the ladder over three years in the product development department of a technology company, rising to the level of liaison with the marketing and IT divisions. This was back in the days when the internet was firing up and companies were trying to develop a "web presence".

Her company decided that they needed a stunning web site in order to attract a merger offer, and so she was assigned to hire an external candidate. Her boss, Sam, says he's been sent a resume of a "*hot designer*" from an ex-colleague and so the designer was of course interviewed.

Though it was against policy to bypass HR, Sam instructed Cheryl to meet this young woman first and, if they both liked her, they would not send a position request down to HR.

Cheryl thought there might be something off about Jessica because her resume was extravagant, but Cheryl's boss pushed hard for Jessica to be hired. So she was hired and negotiated her compensation with Sam. Cheryl was in charge monitoring the department budget and nearly died when she realized how much Jessica was being paid: about $130,000 per year - without a college degree.

Web designers were in serious demand at the time and knew they could command high salaries, but Cheryl made around half that much and she told herself that Jessica had better be the hotshot Sam thought she was.

And so Jessica gets to work, well sort of: a month goes by, no web site. A second month goes by and though Jessica shows up and sits at her desk, she claims that she is not being given "*enough guidance*" to accomplish the task.

Cheryl then is asked quietly by Sam to step in and take over *all* of the project management. Cheryl is a team player so she agrees to do so, but she is angered because she knows that the budget on the project was fixed. Sam shows no signs of getting rid of Jessica and Cheryl won't get paid any more. There will be some needed overtime to bring the project back on schedule, but because she is a manager, she is classified as exempt for overtime pay. Sam hints at a bonus, but Cheryl's heard that before.

Cheryl realizes, after about 3 days of working more closely with Jessica that she is a scammer and that she does not know much about web programming. When confronted, Jessica says that she thought the job was graphic design and not very much web.

Cheryl goes to Sam with this information and though Sam agrees that Jessica probably can't get it done, instead of firing Jessica, Sam asks Cheryl to see if Tony and Renee in IT know anything about web design and programming. Unfortunately for their weekend plans, it turns out that they have been taking HTML as part of continuing education, and so Sam assigns them to this growing team.

Amazingly, Sam still glows about Jessica to others around the office: *Jessica will get it done and we're going to have a cutting edge presence on the net. Just you wait and see! It will be money well invested!*

Cheryl tries not to roll her eyes at these mid-meeting outbursts. She decides that Sam is trying to convince himself that things will be fine because it's a high profile project and he does not want his leadership questioned.

Tony and Renee spend weeks tweaking all the bugs Jessica created and still the website does not seem to work as expected. It takes 9 months until Sam has a moderately decent site, but it is only because Tony and Renee finally re-program the site from scratch.

Then the 9/11 tragedy occurs. There is an immediate panic in the business world. Within weeks, the senior executives have decided that layoffs are needed. The huge stock market drop rattles nerves and six people in Cheryl's department are rapidly let go. She keeps her job and so does, believe it or not, *Jessica*.

Through the layoffs, a rather key position is vacated laterally to Cheryl and Sam promotes Jessica into the job, a job that normally would require more education, starting at somewhat lower pay. Many are in shock, and whispers start about Jessica having done the "*horizontal hustle*" to get the job.

But look, gossip like this starts when employees observe incomprehensible decisions made by their managers. Sam seems completely oblivious to the fact that now Jessica will be supervising people with far more experience than she has. If she were an older worker, it would not matter so much that she does not have a college degree, for experience would be more in play, but now Jessica is supervising at least one person with a master's degree and that person was overlooked when the rapid promotion was done.

As Cheryl put it,

"All hell broke loose after that. Jessica had no managerial training whatsoever and yet shockingly they expected her to know how to supervise and manage veteran employees. She was the laughing-stock of the company, but Sam kept her on."

Jessica's ineptitude finally got up the chain of command after she coerced some hourly staff to work after hours on a project that she was doing for an outside client. The Payroll Manager noticed a high level of overtime and, by policy, it was brought to the CFO's attention.

Jessica was finally "negotiated out" after 15 months of creating total chaos. With trust broken, because they also found out that Sam bypassed HR policies, Sam was let go through layoff, and so was Cheryl, because she was seen as Sam's loyal staffer on the web site project that cost double the budget due to additional staff time required by the project

So much for helping out the boss.

This void in character is perhaps the most common scenario most people will have to face. It's often hard to do anything about it because the people below manager Sam have no access to the folks above Sam to discuss what is going on. But Sam and Jessica do not care, because the story that Cheryl found out later was that Jessica was the step-daughter of Sam's brother.

and they remained family

happily ever after

Need I say more?

STORY 4: REFERENCES

NOTE: This story relies upon the heavily researched psychological frameworks both of Dr. George Simon, Jr. in the book, "*In Sheep's Clothing: Understanding and Dealing with Manipulative People*" and of Dr. Paul Babiak and Dr. Robert Hare in "*Snakes in Suits: When Psychopaths Go To Work*". In my opinion, both books are worth a serious read to anyone trying to understand what might seem like unexplainable events in the workplace.

* *

John tells the following complex story about his friend Paul. John had worked with Paul and said that Paul is a hardworking, ethical employee any business would be happy to have on board. So, some background:

Terri was hired as the Chief Financial Officer for a Not-For-Profit. She worked for a CEO named Betty, who had been with the organization for several years. Betty was probably someone who could get a clinical diagnosis for being a psychopath. Amongst other things, she fired people whenever they caught her in the lies or the out and out fraud that typically accompanies such a person. I'll talk more about character disordered people through the rest of the book, but for now, consider that clinical psychopaths have no normal conscience to speak of.

CFO Terri soon learned that she had to work around Betty to keep within the law and GAAP accounting rules, but after a couple years, Terri finally found herself at the end of Betty's gun after Terri informed Betty that one of her directives was illegal. Terri was immediately terminated by Betty, but Terri fought back and listed all the dirt she had on Betty that she would take to the Board unless Betty made a deal: pay Terri for 6 months on the clock, including benefits, and she would go quietly.

Betty was finally cornered, but she made the terms of the deal such that Terri would not show up for work, so almost no one would know and it would not look as though Betty had been out-maneuvered. This deal was kept from most, if not all, of the Board of Directors. It was no wonder that some people apparently called the agency "*Betty's Lair*". Some people had wondered how Betty was able to stay in power, but nothing was done to remove her even though two official complaints of harassment had been filed with the Board over the past 5 years.

So CFO Terri was gone, but that's just the backdrop and we'll soon see how Terri offers a clear example of character deficit as well. According to John, it was a complex situation, so keep in mind that the main theme here is that CFO Terri endeavored to damage the reputation of John's friend Paul, who worked at the agency after Terri "left"; Terri accomplished this deed by telling Paul's recruiter false and / or highly distorted information, and we'll get to how that happened, but first:

Upon hire, Paul saw the 6 month agreement that Betty had made with Terri. He was responsible to authorize payroll and the Deputy Director filled him in over a long lunch, so he had the information about what had happened.

Now Paul had not worked for Terri before, but Terri found a way to slander Paul's reputation based on comments made by a friend, Board Member Ned.

Board Member Ned served with Terri on an entirely different Environmental Not-For-Profit Board of Directors and through that separate connection, Terri heard that Ned had some opinions about Paul. *How*? Because Ned liked being on boards and so *also* sat on the board of the agency Paul had left *before* coming to Betty's Lair: "*the Agency of Religious Hypocrites*".

*So by now you are probably asking: how was CFO Terri able to reach out to Paul's recruiter since **she** had been terminated from Betty's Lair?*

Well, like the three predecessors before him in the role, Paul found problems that could not be denied should the outside CPA auditor ask. In this case, after a few months, Paul found forged financial documents that Betty the probable psychopath executed. Betty found out from her administrative assistant that Paul knew of the forgeries and after a confrontation, Paul voluntarily left, with a huge severance package and an agreement to not disclose any illegal actions done by Betty.

But this time the Board found out that Betty made a deal with Paul and that she had cut two very large checks out of the payroll system so as to bypass a required approval of large checks.

A couple board members had become suspicious as another complaint about Betty had been submitted in just the prior 6 months, but now they had physical evidence. So after letting a couple more months pass so as to not openly link the board decision directly to Paul's situation, they subsequently fired Betty.

Yet instead of admitting that there had been an injustice done to Paul, a highly qualified manager with good references who might have become CFO, the agency instead re-hired the not so ethical *Terri* in an interim role. And so, according to John, this is how CFO Terri came to be in contact at all with the recruiting firm, since Paul's position was now open.

So when Terri spoke to the recruiter to permanently place someone in Paul's old position, John said she violated the Betty's Lair handbook on what information can be disclosed, as she had no supervisory relationship with Paul, and he had not authorized her to talk with the recruiter about him.

According to the psychologists mentioned at the front of this story, people with character disorders have no problem spreading unfounded dirt, if only perhaps to undercut an occupational competitor from future work opportunities.

As a result, probably because the agency was a good client since they had very high staff turnover, the <u>recruiter</u> was somehow persuaded to *believe* unsubstantiated accusations about Paul that had originated with Ned the Board Member.

John said that Paul told him he was unable to obtain any other placements from the recruiter, even though Paul's *prior supervisor on a different contract* though the recruiter had given him a stellar recommendation.

In short, Terri made a conscious and concerted effort to slander Paul's reputation, with blatant disregard for employment law, and at least to some extent, her efforts seem to have worked.

What!? you ask, *how can this be so*?

Well, it happens, and Paul will also probably be prevented from any decent jobs in the Not-For-Profit sector in that entire community, as, since Paul has come to learn, some people in the sector break employment laws and the organizations often <u>share</u> board members.

In my opinion, this story is not as likely to occur in For-Profits; people in business understand that some places are just not good fits. Though admittedly it happens there too, I believe it's generally seen as *petty* and strong evidence of character deficit on the part of *the gossiper*.

AGENCY OF THE RELIGIOUS HYPOCRITES

So, you may ask, *why had Paul left the Agency of the Religious Hypocrites where the gossip came from in the first place?*

Was anything that Board Member Ned ranted to CFO Terri about even remotely true about Paul?

No. According to John, there had been very **illegal** goings on by the Board and the CEO at the religious agency, ones that were even worse than those happening at *Betty's Lair* and Paul had simply been required to report what he saw.

And how did Paul find out about CFO Terri telling the recruiter?

Well, believe it or not, the recruiter was so inured to any potential legal consequences that she just told Paul outright what Terri had said. I mean, what's Paul going to do? Sue the recruiter who holds access to future potential jobs?

And how did Paul find out that it was almost certainly Board Member Ned who told CFO Terri the lies about Paul?

The recruiter told Paul straight out that CFO Terri said that the information came from "a friend" on the Board of the Religious Hypocrites.

So Ned was identified because Paul easily checked and saw that Terri and Ned are friends on Facebook and that no other board members were observably befriended by Terri. Then Paul searched the internet and found out they were both on the Environmental Not-For-Profit's Board of Directors together.

Ergo, it was Ned.

According to John's telling, Board Member Ned had apparently broken several laws while Paul worked at the religious Not-For-Profit agency, including aiding and abetting in the illegal firing of a young African American and the illegal cover up that followed.

But clearly, by telling CFO Terri *anything* about Paul at all, Ned the Board Member also broke any potential legal agreement between Paul and the Agency of the Religious Hypocrites for confidentiality. I also believe that Ned probably broke whatever reference giving language would have been in their employment handbook, since that sort of language is fairly standard now: title, pay, and period of employment.

Further, Board Members of any organization are not supposed to disclose any information about employees **at all** (unless it's the CEO and they are the Chair) and so Ned was outside the legal scope of his role.

So do you think Board Member Ned cared that his lies and gossip may have hurt Paul?

No, according to John, Ned was a retired government employee who apparently to like to sit on boards to wield some power and probably thinks there is no way anyone can retaliate. He is likely wrong if he thinks that's the case, as Paul could have filed a suit against him for defamation and Ned would not have been protected by the organization's attorneys. Paul could have also filed the same kind of suit against CFO Terri, and perhaps he did so.

Unfortunately, from stories I have heard, and my own experience suggests, people on Not-For-Profit boards can be blindly arrogant because they actually believe that they are somehow "on top". They have also seen little or no consequences meted out for such disclosures, and so they blab, because "*what's in it for them*" is to try to assign blame to other people in order to deflect any attention away from their own illegal actions, should anything *later* come out to donors or the general public.

In sum, I believe the gossiping is often **conscious** *pre-emptive back-stabbing* by character deficient people.

In the case above, John said that Paul related that Board Member Ned had been engaged in illegal activities, and so we can see that there is a motive for Ned's ranting about Paul to CFO Terri that has *nothing* to do with Paul's capabilities.

Do you think the recruiter will ever get the real story?

Well, if Paul did sign a confidentiality agreement with the Agency of the Religious Hypocrites, he can't mitigate Terri's slander by telling the recruiter what happened there without violating an agreement, now can he?

Paul is therefore in little position to defend himself from the void in character behavior of people like Board Member Ned and CFO Terri; after all, a board member would never *lie*, right?

Wrong! They have millions of dollars of incentive to lie and we'll look into more of that later.

What's worse? Stories from others and my experience say that Terri and Ned get juiced by Paul's victimization; they may get together, drink cocktails and brag about how they showed that dumb-o Paul a thing or two. In sum, I believe the Terri's and Ned's of this world use their positions of petty power to exert undue influence in lots of directions that have *nothing* to do with the missions of their organizations; *it's simply for their own enjoyment.*

And I also believe that it's 99% likely that if character deficient people think they see themselves described here, they will hide under the rock they crawled out from under. They are typically cowards and the average character deficient CFO Terri, Board Member Ned, or recruiter, in my experience, only try these things if they think they can get away it.

My bias is that I find these sorts of stories revealing but disgusting, and it's even more repulsive when it's like Paul's situation. Being Board Members somewhere, Ned and Terri are *expected to know* employment laws and so it's clear from John's telling that these people colluded, knowingly breaking laws to slander someone who John said was only following the rules. What's even more hideous to me is that they are typically the kind of folks who have no problem lying under oath and then sleeping just fine that night.

Further, for CFO Terri, what she probably did not consider was that she has clearly indicated to the recruiter that *she herself* is not trustworthy as a candidate, and, since the recruiter is not absolutely ethical either, what would prevent the recruiter from refusing to place Terri, should *Betty's Lair* decide to force her out again?

Nothing, and this story shows just how short-sighted people with character deficits can be. Certainly CFO Terri could have received immediate repercussions if the Board at *Betty's Lair* were told what Terri did to violate Paul's severance package, but according to John, Paul believes he should just move on, since God knows how many of those board members *also* have slanderous diarrhea of the mouth.

My opinion: people like Ned, Terri, and Betty are **prime carriers** of the disease that is weakening and perhaps completely poisoning our ability to trust one another in daily life: apathy, character deficit, breaking of each other's employment rights, rounded out with large doses of "*what's in it for me?*".

NOT-FOR-PROFIT COVER UPS

The last story is a bit of a hint of what's to come later in this book, but one of the problems we face is that honest people of good character like Paul do not see this coming. The employee handbooks say one thing in black and white and the Not-For-Profit Boards operate differently, often in *direct contradiction* with the specific language in the handbooks.

Why? Because employment lawyers tell the Boards they can, and in fact, my research and my experience indicates that they inform them that it is *their responsibility to protect the organization first* and so, lawyers recommend the Board kick out employees who just do not get *how it really works,* and then, the lawyers help the Boards kick them out.

And why do Boards blatantly ignore employment handbook language?

Because, in my opinion, a lot of the funding would dry up if people knew how often bad stuff like this happens in Not-For-Profits.

My question: *Shouldn't a Not-For-Profit be allowed to fail, like businesses often do, if run by incompetent or law-breaking management?*

For the capitalist, this is how nature takes care of business incompetency, and yet here we have unnatural forces in play, propping up very incompetent managers engaging in what I believe are pernicious patterns of illegal activity.

To close this chapter, recently another friend told me they had heard second hand of a CFO for a Not-For-Profit who embezzled $250,000. Though they *breached their fiduciary duty* by not watching closely enough, the Board decided not to report it or file charges because they did not want negative publicity to impact donations.

If they choose to go that way, shouldn't the Board members themselves then pay it back?

Embezzlement in Not-For-Profits happens far more often than you might think; the amount is not tremendous in all cases, but I worked in one years ago where the Office Manager embezzled about $10,000 using agency credit cards; she was promptly fired, but a police report was not filed.

And so do you think that just perhaps there should be a Not-For-Profit law that requires:

1) **Disclosure** in the Form 990, the financial, and/or the audit reports of any employment exit agreement that requires confidentiality beyond the normal handbook language, particularly if the agreement is with financial staff as they have access to funds.

2) **Reporting** of *any* embezzlement or potential crime to the local District Attorney's office and any relevant state licensure agency with

heavy fines if not reported, plus major penalties if there is a delay of more than 30 days between identification of a potential crime and when it is reported.

3) Further, do you think perhaps there should be the creation of an anonymous hotline for employees or others to report potential crimes or delays in reporting to the DA's office?

You decide.

My opinion:

Not-For-Profits receive a unique exemption from taxes and they should have to be transparent in return, and, yes, after some years dealing with them, I believe we need transparency with *MUCH* stronger teeth. As *over 15%* of our workforce now works in Not-For-Profits, I contend the public should want to know a lot more about what is going on in those organizations.

I have a lot more to say later about these organizations, but basically it comes down to this: I am not talking about the Kaisers and Special Olympics of the world. While most of the larger ones *are* well-run, I believe there are far too many other smaller ones that may be acting as little more than a vehicle for the dysfunctional activities of an untrained and/or character disordered leader who has been allowed to run amuck.

And one of the main reasons I think it is important that Americans get our expectations about Not-For-Profits clarified is that *character* becomes far more critical as we look to the area where a good number of people in our country believe Not-For-Profits should take an even more active role: *Healthcare*.

HEALTHCARE

IT'S A COGNITIVE DISSONANCE PROBLEM

So if you believe that Not-For-Profits should take on a bigger role in healthcare as a way to help manage down costs, and many do, we also have other issues to contend with, and we need to bring those issues into this broadening conversation.

I believe that America's healthcare issues create cognitive dissonance for just about everyone involved. Questions of who gets care and at what level are conflicting for most people because when it comes down to it, we all want the best care for ourselves but, if *push came to shove, it's okay for your family to have less quality care than mine. It's just the way it is.*

But even if that seems like an easy conclusion, typically, there's something about *thinking* that way that is very unsettling and creates dissonance. Most of us feel basic healthcare is a basic need; we are taught that growing up.

Children's story books will often carry a theme in them that if you have an injury, you go to the doctor. The stories do not say: *if you have insurance and have an injury, then you go to the doctor; if you don't have insurance, try the county emergency room*. But that's how it is right now.

I am going to try to avoid numbers as much as possible, as for me, the numbers are what make it all so mind-numbing, and my tendency is to turn off the dialogue. This book is about elevating the dialogue, not becoming another sack of data. And the numbers are also what the politicians use to polarize the dialogue about health care.

However, while I refer you to the internet if you want more data, we do need a few key numbers to get our heads around the situation:

- Healthcare comprises about $1 in every $6 dollars in the gross domestic product (GDP). In other words, about 16 cents out of every dollar spent is involved in healthcare spending.

- 14% of the Federal budget goes to Medicare and a total of 21% of the budget goes into healthcare spending; Medicare is expected to increase to over 20% in the next decades.

- According to Harvard researchers, in 2007, 62% of personal bankruptcies were due to healthcare costs.

What these numbers tell us is that we just can't ignore the magnitude of the impact of healthcare in our economy, and, that the current state of affairs is hurting a lot of people.

To this centrist Joe, if at all possible, all Americans should have *access* to basic healthcare, but it simply is not possible for everyone to have everything they ever want through government policies, and that includes high end boutique healthcare (optional plastic surgery, the newest technological intervention, or *avant garde* procedures).

My reasons for this view, though, are not simplistic, and so this conversation needs to bring in an example. Now I am no expert in healthcare insurance: what is covered and what is not, for whom and when.

Who could be? It changes from company to company, plan to plan, state to state and so on. So we're going to try to keep this conversation top level and focused on the main issues that drive the conflicted emotions about it. And so first, I want to make a primary point before I try to take a more balance approach through this mine field.

My opinion (and it's a fact too):

No matter what any of us do

we do not get out of life alive.

THE PATIENT

Hannah feels sick and so goes to the doctor's office. Her doctor sees some odd findings and orders a blood test, which shows an elevated blood count; with some additional confirmatory tests, Hannah is told that she has cancer. The doctor's prognosis is that Hannah only has 6 months to live without immediate intervention.

The doctor tells her that the alternative is 12 months tops if Hannah wants to seek out some cutting edge interventions that will cost her and the insurance company $150,000 in chemotherapy, surgery, and hospital stays.

Which does Hannah choose? Well, as anyone connected even indirectly to a situation involved in these things, it's not a simple question. Basically, should Hannah wish to pursue an additional six months of life, it's not just her decision: the insurance company has a say in it. So who is to blame if Hannah finds she's not freely able to choose the 12 month option without the rigmarole of pre-approvals?

It's no one's fault and it's everyone's fault. Now there are people who rip on insurance companies because they do what they can to minimize costs (someone else's book), but it is no one person's fault for the healthcare quagmire, and I believe it is everyone's responsibility to fix it. At the same time, it is also true that it is antithetical to capitalism to require the insurers to pay for every procedure desired; after all, like most doctors and hospitals, insurers are businesses too and are in it to make a profit.

This is part of why most of us all confused about it, and I'd hazard that probably no one fully trusts the numbers from either political party, as there are just too many special interest groups that highly influence those figures.

But what I do think is that somehow medical care keeps going up when so many other expenses in our lives (other than education) have stagnated or have dropped. How does that happen?

There was an article I read in about 2010, in which a physician detailed out that something like an average of 70 tests are given to each Medicare patient should they come in with a complaint. He also claimed that there was excessive hospitalization because that's what gets reimbursed. His conclusion was that the financial incentives in healthcare are to do more intervention, not less, and so cost containment suffers.

I think most of us suspect that maybe some people do not want you to go home and die peacefully in bed. We suspect that there are people out there who wish to squeeze every last dollar out of a person's estate, and it is set up that way because in part, the doctor and hospitals get paid by ordering more, not less, having you be in the hospital more, not less.

And if you suspect that this is so, then *the insurance companies* are the only force in some cases, that are preventing doctors and hospitals from taking all of your assets in the name of *making you comfortable* or giving you longer to come to terms with your pending mortality.

Had you ever thought of insurance that way?

Maybe not, so I'll say it differently: The insurance companies may be saving your children's inheritance by saying no to the hot shot doctor who wants to try out her new technique on you when it's clear you are in your last six months of life.

Also, if you think about it: when grandpa is taking 20 different pills every day, he is probably consuming more meds than all four of his grandparents did in their entire life - **combined** - and they lived and then died just fine without all those chemicals doing God knows what.

But that's progress, right? Well, certainly it's scientific progress, and even if we're a bit confused about whether or not it could be another type of progress, what we all do know is that the cost to stay alive is more expensive now.

Is it wrong? I am not sure. In this country, we believe that if someone's grandfather wants to spend all his money on medication he can. I am not suggesting that we should all die at home, or even refuse treatment. I am saying that it just seems to most of us like it all costs too much, period.

But people have cognitive dissonance about it because it's very emotional stuff, and I believe this is what keeps many people in a quandary about how far to go with reform, what government's role should be, and where socialized medicine fits in, if at all. It also becomes complicated for a lot of people because it is not socially acceptable to come across to anyone that we are uncaring about healthcare, even to most of those with voids in character.

Still, the cost projections for the future are clear: if we do not want to backflip into the debt pool every year, we need to contain these costs, as they are a huge part of the Federal budget, with 21% of it going to healthcare spending for 2011.

So, I am not sure "Obamacare" will always work or work well, but does anyone have a better idea that is not just a "what's in it for me?" solution for one special interest group or another?

Just asking.

ANOTHER TWIST TO CONSIDER

So even if a person is not dying or suffering from a physical ailment, there are a lot of people relying on the healthcare sector to make it through their day.

As of 2005, an estimated *10%* of the American population was taking psychotropic medication said an *Archives of General Psychiatry* study. The National Institute of Mental Health states that about 26% of Americans over 18 are diagnosable as having at least one psychiatric disorder each year, with 5.8% considered severe.

This is an important statistic for us to understand: 26%, or over one quarter of Americans, are mentally suffering in one way or another in any given year. 10% of the population on psychotropic medication is literally like 33+ million people. New data released in late 2011 states that **20%** are now on psychotropics. That implies that perhaps one in five people you know is medicated, maybe on Prozac or Zoloft, and another maybe one in 20 could be on something else. And so I ask:

- *If so many are depressed, why do you think that could be?*

- *Could it in part be due to the dysfunctional things that happen at work?*

- *Did you know that one well known side effect of the drug Zoloft is* **apathy?**

- *Could Zoloft be why at least a few people you know have an apathetic reaction to bad behavior?*

- *Could this psychotropic medication trend be part of the reason character deficit (and the apathy towards it) seems to be taking hold in our country?*

You decide.

And what else might be keeping our conflict about healthcare in play besides fear of dying and medicating for mental discomfort? There are many other reasons why, and not only political ones, that make change hard to bring into effect.

In fact, there are a lot of people who are just fine with healthcare the way it is because they assume they will always have coverage - OR - they work in healthcare and make a good living because of the way things are - OR - there are economic benefits that come in another way...

for there is another piece to this pie.

BUT DO I *NEED* ANOTHER TEST?

My friend Risa has worked in healthcare for many years. Risa tells the story that she has always been astonished at the testing equipment some hospitals would replace within a few years. It was bragging rights for the doctors and the administrators: We got a bigger, newer, more advanced, less invasive, *more stainless steel machine that you do. It's so big we need a new wing to put it in. Hey guys, what big shot can we get to donate that kind of money? We'll tell them their family name will live on in infinity on the building - where is that Marketing Officer anyway!?*

So Risa's view of Hannah, the cancer patient, is that if her doctor ordered it, she probably would be authorized to get a battery of tests on the brand new machine, and the results would inform her doctor that Hannah probably has one extra week to live, statistically speaking, beyond the 6 months. So, was the test needed?

Well, the battery of tests cost $10,000, fully loaded for hospital overhead. What is not so well understood, even in "non-profit" managed care health care systems, is that the doctor often participates in a "risk pool", in other industries called "profit sharing". That is, they don't just obtain profits from their practice, they also get them from how they use the hospital's services.

Risa agrees with me that risk pools are not a bad idea in theory, since if the doctors "over-order" tests, they get less of the pooled profit. But what's not so public in the first place is that profits from tests are funneled back to the doctors at the end of the year. So Risa told me that for a $10,000 test, the physician bonus pool probably would receive about $500 that the doctor would share with 49 other docs (keeping it simple).

If there are another 49 tests run on the machine, another $24,500 goes into that risk pool. So while the doctors can be individually penalized for "over-use", they benefit from ordering tests within a range. Now clearly, each one of them probably orders hundreds of tests each on the machine yearly, so that "risk pool" can get large.

And is there really any *risk*? Well, perhaps not a whole lot.

If you were shown by the sales representative how many tests you needed to do a year in order to have the biggest, best, most modern cancer detecting equipment possible, and if you were guaranteed the Federal government would pay for every test you order through Medicare, and if insurance companies do not have the test flagged as a major pre-approval item, then that minimizes a lot of the risk in buying the machine.

But according to Risa, what happens is that doctors go to conventions and next year's model of the test equipment is sitting there, looking shinier and more prestigious - and the profit margin, the sales reps tell the doctors, make this machine far more attractive. The sales reps then show them exactly how much cash will flow into the doctor's "risk pool" at various levels of usage and so, they are motivated to trade them in - hence a hidden factor in healthcare that is not in the public's conversation.

Ok, so that's Risa's view, but it looks like there may be a change of heart. A Bain & Company survey reached out to 300 doctors at all ages and ranges of experience in a report called "*The new cost-conscious doctor: Changing America's healthcare landscape*".

As Bain states, "*for the first time a majority of physicians show an increased willingness to consider the cost implications of the products they use. They recognize a pressing need to adjust their clinical practices to accommodate healthcare cost considerations*".

This is a promising new awareness for us as tax-payers, but even if the doctors move in this direction in a big way, and while the report indicates that the equipment vendors will see drops in sales, these vendors are still very large players.

And I contend that they, and the pharmaceutical companies, should be big players: we need equipment and we need medication. For what it is they provide, really the issue is *how much* equipment and *how much* medication and at what price. But when we talk vendors, we have to bring in the stock market, as most of the big vendors are publicly traded corporations, and that reality influences the health care debate - *a lot.*

THE STOCK MARKET

Who else does not want a whole lot of control put on medical expenses?

Wall Street and, to some extent, me.

While someone on Wall Street might try to argue that increasing healthcare costs are a huge drain, the fact is that 1) lower *wages* internationally are the big factor in competitiveness and 2) if all American companies face about the same costs for healthcare, then there is no company-specific risk due to health care that other companies do not also face. Together, these facts suggest the non-competitive argument has a specious smell to it.

However, that healthcare costs rise a lot is a problem if there are few forces to constrain them because it suggests monopolistic trends. And while I am unsure about how we can care for all of our elderly on a baseline level without change, here's the source of my dissonance: I do not want to be dependent on Social Security later, particularly since I may not receive benefits at the same level my parents have.

But here's the rub: it is difficult to grow a retirement nest egg without at least some good dividend paying stocks and healthcare related stocks pay some of the largest and most solid dividends out there. In part, it is because the prices for healthcare can currently be mostly passed along to the consumer: patients and their third party payers (insurance and government).

My question: *what would take the place of the healthcare stocks in a diversified retirement portfolio?*

Small investors, large investors, and endowment funds buy these stocks *in droves*. Pension plans do too, and so the weight of their needs to meet current and future obligations could be impacted if the high profits that turn into high income streams through dividend payments were taken away.

The pension plans might feel pressure to invest in more risky stocks and there is evidence, exposed by the recent banking debacle, that pension plans may have investment committees who are not the sharpest knives in the drawer, so *changes could have unthought-about risks to the taxpayer should we have to pick up the gap if solid dividend paying stocks are impaired by healthcare price control.*

And *this* is where a lot of the opposition to Obamacare has come from. Even if you can handle most of the ideas of Obamacare, often your average Joe has money in the game and that causes mental conflict about *"what's in it for me?".*

Keeping it real, because of the looming Medicare burden, I hate to be the messenger, but the math alone suggests that we are going to see a move towards even more universal care, probably along the lines of what they have in Canada, and probably in about 20 years, give or take 5 years.

Fortunately, due to so many complaints, Canada is starting guaranteed maximum wait times for specific procedures. They see it as a work in progress, but what's true is that Americans may simply not stand for 3 - 6 month waiting periods, so should I be prescient, there will probably be a huge increase in the demand here for Physician Assistants and for Nurse Practitioners to handle everything but what a doctor needs to review or diagnose.

Moving down the skill range for basic primary care may help cost containment while still allowing for continued robust healthcare dividends, so is this model a bad idea? I am not sure we'll have a choice, but if it does occur as I am presenting it, I am sure that a schedule can be established so that Physician Assistants and Nurse Practitioners would know when to refer someone to a full blown doctor.

As for other interventions and surgeries, particularly for those that might be called *elective*, it is more complicated for us because it dovetails into a discussion of the American Dream.

So here's my question: *Is a knee replacement surgery a quality of life issue so that the kids do not have to be "burdened" with grandma coming to live with them or is it truly a **need** for the person?*

I personally do not have a clear answer for myself. Would I want the surgery? Not sure, as I have heard mixed results about knee and hip surgery. Some people do great for a few years and then the knees fail again, *so what's the truth*?

Again, the truth is that the human body has a life-span, its parts wear out, and then you pass on.

But if I had a strong sense that the surgery would work, then probably I'd go for it if I were still shy of 70, assuming it's available to me at a price I can afford. Do I think when harder choices will have to be made about healthcare that this is the sort of surgery that will be considered solely elective? Yes, probably.

The middle-upper class and rich will still be able to get these sorts of procedures done, at least partially out of pocket. Just about everything surgical is possible for people with money and so it will be the poor and middle class where the elective surgery decision will be made, *for them*, with the argument being that it is for the economic benefit of the country as a whole. And quite frankly, maybe it will be.

We're not going to solve this question here, but my point is to raise the topic in a different way, to be at least one person who admits that they have conflicted feelings that have *nothing* to do with some politico-philosophical argument: **it's about my retirement assets**. That's why I'm conflicted and I believe that's why a lot of people are conflicted.

Changing how healthcare works could have a big impact on every one of us if we decide that only universal care is the solution. See, the facts are that if we change things so much that it takes away larger healthcare dividends, that retirement portfolio - *the very assets that might make it possible for someone to become a full time volunteer in their 60s* - might not be realizable.

Not all of us want to use wealth to ride around in a sail boat based out of Miami or San Francisco; some of us believe and understand that *what goes around, comes around*. In this view, the nation's debt and other big problems are what are *coming* around due to some questionable decisions that *went* around.

So, probably like you, I am conflicted about what is best and hope not too many of my investing opportunities will be taken away. But I am willing to take a chance and I find myself hoping that Obamacare remains in place, if only so that we see what this experiment will do, because something preventative had to be done.

Again, if not Obamacare, then what?

I believe that healthcare is one topic where we can easily see that high school finance would have helped Americans have a better dialogue and that the lack of math knowledge has helped politicians and others polarize the debate.

Maybe Obamacare will keep enough of the old system in place so that the growth in my wealth is not stifled; but maybe it won't and I will have to adjust; no matter what, we'll all need to watch diligently for what comes next.

And regardless of that potential future, one of the main conflicts people have when thinking about the business of healthcare is that executives in health care (and other sectors, to be fair) take home high levels of compensation such that their complaints when even minor price containment is proposed seem disingenuous, and so I feel we need to bring *executive pay* into the larger character conversation.

COMPENSATION
AND PHILANTHROPY

First and foremost, I do not know if a CEO of a publicly traded company should receive $1 million+ stock awards or a flat $10 million per year or something different entirely.

Executive Pay was debated in business school: *how much is appropriate? How much is too much?*

There was no clear answer; most students felt there should be some equity vertically but there was the assumption that more compensation should go to those who added more *economic value.* These discussions were held before huge gaps in pay emerged, but regardless, I believe that it is just common sense to know that financial rewards will not be distributed equally.

Now who adds more value is sometimes rather "subjectively assigned but objectively measured", as in one person gets a great compensation package when coming in, with a bonus based on how an entire division does; whereas another may come up through the ranks and so gets caught in some arcane HR policy, and so receives a smaller bonus even if his division performs the best on paper. It happens.

And as we saw in Chapter 3, the CEO in the Software Blunder moved a project deadline in an effort to *game* the company's reward system in his favor. If you recall, in response the IT team pushed through a buggy product in order to obtain their bonuses and hence "denied" the CEO an increase in stock awards.

So we see that it can be a complicated game, compensation, and when you add in people with voids in character, who do not care if other people obtain the American Dream and will create an unfair playing field just to ensure theirs, those behaviors provide a large backdrop against which publicly traded executive CEO pay can be seen.

Add to that the fact that some people have experienced being manipulated out of what they felt they were originally promised when they started a new job, and so they see high Executive Pay as an sign of the malicious intent to not *pay fairly*.

The issue for most of those who are upset about Executive Pay is that they believe there is now some serious distortion in *value added* in many publicly traded companies. It has been compounded by the state of the economy, as when so many are suffering due to layoffs, in part due to overseas outsourcing, Executive Pay has remained high; as such, people do not perceive CEOs as "*sharing the pain*".

Interesting here is an article by G. William Donhoff called "*Interlocking Directorates in the Corporate Community*" (2005) in which he discusses the connections of rather a small group people who comprise a good percentage of those who serve on the boards of the largest companies in America. Board members can make $500,000 a year or so for sitting on several boards, and if they are on several boards, they are more likely to be selected for government panels, which in turn give them access to power, which is important to understand when thinking in an integrated manner about America.

The main takeaway at this point is that the Board negotiates and approves the compensation for the CEO, who may also serve with them on a Not-For-Profit board. In a nut shell, these connections can be kind of incestuous, as Board Member Ned and CFO Terri showed in the last chapter.

And, I think it is justifiable to ask if Boards are really being fair if they use "*what I get paid at **my** job*" as the main criterion on which CEO pay stands. It's a little more complicated than that because they do run salary surveys, but the critics' argument has been that this is how they raised pay so high: they spiraled it higher every year by incremental bumps to their peers at other firms, so when the survey came back around in a year or so, the pay package for all those being surveyed was higher.

Now I do not believe this inflation in pay happened at the level of a *conscious* conspiracy discussed at the gym, but they are probably happier to see one another should they cross paths in Vail.

However, in case you think I might be defending the whole shebang, as a point of contrast I take the stance that as far as the Wall Street banking firms go, that they returned to virtually the same bonus system that was in place before the recent debacle was totally unjustified given the damage they had done. I think most people feel that there is a clear character deficit problem in that subsector of the market.

But perhaps attention to it has triggered some improvement. As Reuters Canada reported in "*Wall Street targets pay as trading revenue fizzles*" on July 7, 2011, Wall Street has been "*overhauling pay practices over the past 2-1/2 years to better align incentives with risk. Banks have lifted base salaries, deferred bonus payments and introduced clawback provisions to protect against trades and deals that seem profitable at first, but may later go awry.*"

This trend protects investors as well as the banks, and since this article goes on to say that they are also reducing bonuses, perhaps there is a growing awareness that some change needs to happen.

WORK IT, GAME IT, BUT PAY ME

So currently, we have lots of people who do not perceive that CEOs add *that* much more value than other employees, particularly when so many have been let go. If you add the facts of the Wall Street banking debacle then you have a lot of people who are pretty angry about Executive Pay, no matter their political affiliation.

However, before we go into some ironies about it, I still would be the first person to support the position that a CEO brings high levels of strategic value to a corporation and should be paid very well for it.

Why? In my opinion, having been an owner of more than one successful business, this is one of those times where the average person just does not understand for a moment the pressure and responsibility a CEO can feel for his or her people.

First, let's be clear, some CEOs do bad things; some like to call that "shrewd" to make it sound less improper, but keeping it real, some probably did get where they are through underhanded or illegal actions.

That said, most great CEOs see themselves as caretakers of the company, its people, and its resources. For all of the privately held CEOs I have known, the definition of "*me*" in the "*What's in it for me?*" is expanded into an enlightened self-interest definition to include the company and its people.

Also, in my experience, CEOs work harder than just about anyone else - they have to in order to keep their finger on the pulse - at least 60 good hours a week. One recent report noted in BusinessBrief, called "*The CEO Time Use Project*", shows that the maximum number of productive hours for a CEO is about 60 hours and that there are diminishing returns thereafter. Maybe the VPs go play golf a couple times a week, but I personally have never seen a CEO "goof off" for more than a couple of hours a month.

Fact is, most CEOs just love to work. Virgin's Richard Branson is a great example. The guy just oozes business and he gets paid to do probably what he'd do even if he weren't getting paid for it. He deserves high compensation; he created thousands of jobs.

And even if you think all CEOs are paid too much, I ask you: *what is fair then?*

An AFL-CIO analysis of data from Salary.com showed that the total comp for a CEO in 299 of the S&P 500 companies averaged $11 million each in 2010. As a result, these CEOs make on average about **343 times** more than the average American worker. That is a huge difference, no doubt, and it's far more than it was back when my schoolmates and I were debating the issue. Back then it was something like 40 times. Some thought that was kind of steep; some, of course, it being an business school, thought the sky was the limit for anyone's pay, as long as you could convince someone to pay you that much.

But now, due to the Dodd-Frank Wall Street Reform and Consumer Protection Act passed in 2010, shareholders have a "say-on-pay" vote to address CEO compensation; it is not binding, but it sends a message to the Board. The companies must also disclose the CEO-to-worker pay ratio and so investors and prospective workers will also be able to evaluate a company on that basis.

My guess is that with public pressure, there will be a flattening of the CEO pay packages, for at least a while, but I think it's worth it to dig a little deeper here on what impact it has had *emotionally* in America to have such large differences emerge.

I contend that many Americans are now angry and think there should be more parity. With the indifference shown in outsourcing, I believe people now simply think that some CEO compensation should be redistributed to create a dozen or so middle class jobs in the company, because I think that's where the primary public grievance is on this issue, that, and *being overworked.*

OVERWORKED

From the average corporate worker's point of view, if they are salaried and exempt from overtime, recent articles have indicated that some businesses now see that as some kind of license to work them 60 hours or more a week. I refer you to a great column that sums up all the ailments involved in overwork called "*The Taboo Toxin Of Overwork*" (Huffington Post, July 12, 2011).

Personally, I am not into overworking people for the extra penny on the dollar it might get a company. Sure my employees had some overtime here and there, but I always liked my employees to smile when they saw me coming, not cringe in fear that they might lose their weekend or be next on the list to cut so the ownership group got an extra 10% to split. I had a longer timeframe than that.

So why are Americans putting up with being turned into serf-type labor? They worry that if they don't, that some unemployed person is willing to take their place and do it instead. Flat out, **it's fear**.

But what's kind of crazy about an insistence on a high number of hours is that some research has shown, and my own experience agrees, that people work beyond about 50 hours, companies get little additional gain per hour, so I say, *why bother*?

People start to do filler activities, or *game it*, if face time is what's rewarded; further, employees begin to suffer from long term fatigue and they start hating their job. But nonetheless, beliefs about success seem to be changing to align with longer hours. To quote an article called "*Top-Level Professionals View 40-Hour Work Week As Part-Time: Report*":

"Many feel, with some justification, that a 40-hour week would be career suicide. This schedule is seen as 'part time' in many professional-managerial jobs, and tends to spell a less-prestigious and less upwardly-mobile career path." (Huffington Post, July 1, 2011)

I contend this is another trend that may have a long term negative impact on America. As other articles have said, and my thoughts are aligned with the blogs written on this topic, *sure*, people may show up at 8 AM to check their email, but then they leave and sneak over to the gym next door, take an hour for lunch, spend 2 hours on the net and email, take at least another 15 minute break for coffee, and a 30 minute dinner before clocking out at 8 PM and waving goodnight to the CEO, trying to make sure they angle their way out of the building to go past her door. Sure, they got in 60 hours *on the clock*, but what the heck did they get done?

And what is the attitudinal result? In my opinion, a far less dedicated work force, because it's been turned into a *game* they mock instead of *work* they feel satisfied in performing; and that's how a lot of people see it: hide and seek with a couple of meetings and deliverables thrown in there for flavor. The net result? In my view, an institutionalization of character void that then spills over into the **work product**.

See, when workers put in 60 hours, but then do not see projects completed, as shown in Chapter 3, this confirms their suspicions that it's all *a big fake drama*. As long as they get most of the work done or the product doesn't kill or otherwise harm, then things are good in the hood; in other words, the slippery slope of character deficit gains a footing in the other functions of the company and so to me, this push for more hours is short sighted thinking.

Hey, you ask, couldn't they unionize to avoid feeling like they have to give into the urge to act badly?

Perhaps, but this is where a lot of Americans dig in their heels, and it's because many people feel that the unions are even more corrupt than business and they are run by people who are interested more in union power and "what's in it for me?" than they are in negotiating _fair_ working terms and conditions.

A lot of people also do not like the tension unionization brings into their work day; and they also do not like the idea that some drug addict can't be exited if he's drooling in his lunch pail all day long and makes no effort to get clean.

So Americans want a fair shake with their employers, but

- if they see what they consider to be excessive compensation at the top,

- if they are forced to work what they know are abusive hours, and

- if there is no implicit job security for a job worked hard since it could be outsourced tomorrow,

they lose trust.

I believe for America to make real headway into our looming problems, we need to be able to trust both the politicians and the workplace community.

The problem right now, as I see it, is when you have an executive mindset that has no problem moving as much as possible overseas without moderating by keeping a chunk of middle class jobs here, and at the same time the wealthy are getting richer, then in fact you are increasing the social gap, and the anger that is emerging should be no surprise; in fact, it should have been predicted.

The most recent debacles have clearly stripped opportunities for wealth, primarily from the middle class, defined basically as people above the working class, but who do not have a Master's degree, a JD, or a CPA license. Instead we see highly disproportionate assets being moved into the corner offices. It has made people feel things are *too far out of balance*.

And even if *you do not care, and you got yours*, what if this out of balance pisses off certain large segments enough so that they start *taking by force* what they were told would be theirs as part of *their* American Dream?

My opinion: just logically, and if you can only justify caring about it for self-preservation reasons, perhaps you should learn a little more about them there Tea Partiers - - yeah, just a tad.

EXECUTIVE PHILANTHROPY??

I think most people know that businesses in America are centrist in their benefit policies, perhaps even a little Left leaning, even though they do not have to be.

Generally, corporations in America have found that it's good business to have a diversified workforce, and even if they are in fact closet racial bigots or homophobes, the work place is a much better place than it was 30+ years ago for minorities of all kinds.

I also think most folks suspect that a lot of CEOs lean Right in their politics. I'd have to agree, and some of them are really very Right, as in Libertarian, which actually can make them less racist and homophobe that you might think, because they think *live and let live* and that the government should stay out of *everything*.

But for many CEOs and high level executives, their goal simply is to amass a fortune and give it to their heirs - and most still go this route. However, there is a current trend to commit to giving fortunes away while people are still living, including the Gates-Buffett Giving Pledge made by 40 billionaires to give at least 50 percent of their wealth away philanthropically. So here's how this Joe see things as it relates to the ironies in this new *Executive Philanthropy*.

ROLL ON THE FLOOR & LAUGH OUT LOUD?

The first ironic part of Executive Philanthropy is that the jobs they create go to the very same kind of people they themselves would *never* hire in a million years in their businesses to run anything, and yet, Executive Philanthropists seem to give them their money blindly.

What many Executive Philanthropists may not understand, because they typically have not worked in the

Not-For-Profit community, is that the people asking for their money are, in my experienced opinion, often master manipulators, perhaps even more manipulative than the Executive ever was.

I have developed this view because, as I've already disclosed to some extent in the Chapter 3 story on References, I have lost a lot of faith in the Not-For-Profit sector's leadership capabilities. After a couple of decades of dealing with these organizations, I now believe that a significant number of those leaders are essentially joyriding on the tailwinds of the hard workers of this country; literally on the very backs of those who helped create the Executive Philanthropist's wealth.

I end up with questions any time I think about this rather surprising, and actually sometimes strange, turn of events. I tell myself that capitalists of either political side will argue that the goal is to make as much as you can and then if you want to give it away to people you would never hire, that's your choice. After all, you earned it "fair and square" (and some did, and some did not, but we're giving the question of executive ethics a rest now).

Admittedly, some have seen the light of this logic, as perhaps they realize that by giving it to employees, they have the potential to create *multiple* future philanthropists. In other words, by giving their company to their employees, they provide a high level example for those families about how to spend money, perhaps *for generations*.

For example, entrepreneur Bob Moore, on his 81st birthday, gave his company, Bob's Red Mill Natural Foods of Oregon, to the people *who brung him*.

I think I can easily defend that most of the time, employees probably deserve it more than the Not-For-Profits who talk Executive Philanthropists into giving them their money, and I'm going to say a lot more about that.

AS IN:

Mr. or Ms. Executive Philanthropist, I have a question:

Why not retrain people you already trust to become your philanthropy team and who might be ready for a different career, than to throw millions or billions at nonprofit careerists who may not know basic HR laws and who mock or otherwise make fun of you - often - *when your back is turned?*

In my years straddling the sectors, most of the Not-For-Profit professionals I knew completely **abhorred** that Executive Philanthropists are capitalists to begin with. I have personally observed a good number of these professionals sit around and laugh at people who are willing to work overtime.

I have additionally observed that the executives often would use their sociological or psychological knowledge to underhandedly appeal to the Executive Philanthropist's ego; the same ego that helped the person amass the money; the same ego that now desires to leave a "lasting legacy".

The truth:

Many Not-For-Profits now have *sophisticated* marketing programs specifically designed to attract High Net Worth prospects: they throw high profile events, they use social networking to create affinity to their cause, they have their board members throw exclusive house parties so that each will know *just* who came and *just* who gave, and they offer Executive Philanthropists opportunities to get their name on a building.

I think we all know that the Executive Philanthropist is smart enough to know this, but still they seem to trust, when again: they never would trust these folks to be members of their corporate staff.

It makes no sense - oh wait, sure it does:

cognitive dissonance

To release the dissonance, many Executive Philanthropists minimize or deny that the Not-For-Profit people ever did not like them. The Executive Philanthropist perhaps tells him or herself that really that they all are on the *same team* to fight whatever the fight might be.

It's that dissipation of the mental conflict that allows Executive Philanthropist to feel okay with handing over a $20 million check because s/he will get a 23 karat gold-leafed sign of their name on a hospital wall "*for posterity's sake*".

Keeping it real, heck, it's almost like having a son and calling him Junior, only this time, Junior's a building.

BUT -

Here's another reason why this interface between For-Profit and Not-For-Profit is important to the future of America, and why the Executive Philanthropist should maybe pay a little bit of attention to what I'm saying: they may not be running their own ships right.

ECONOMIC VALUE AND THE HIDDEN DILEMMA

According to the Council on Nonprofits, more than 10% of the workforce now works in nonprofits and it's increasing *due to philanthropy*. When you add the 5%+ in government workers, that's over 15% of our workforce who work in Not-For-Profits. In other words, that's over 15% of the workforce whose organization pays **no taxes**.

Also, in other words, except in rare cases and in nonprofit healthcare, there is no *return on assets* or ROA. In fact, there is no accepted standard to even calculate an ROA for a Not-For-Profit. For those who are not business people, ROA is defined for a company as "*How many dollars of (**taxable**) earnings they derive from each dollar of assets they control.*" (Wikipedia)

In pure economic terms, that means that the rest of the work force is supplementing these organizations through taxes and donations, and their numbers are growing.

My question: *how can this sort of increasing supplementation last long term?*

It's not that these people do not contribute income tax dollars as employees, but here's something I bet most people do not know: *at least some Not-For-Profits do not pay into Social Security.*

HUH?

Around about 1990, I was told that all Not-For-Profits are **not** required to contribute to Social Security. The IRS website currently says that unless the Not-For-Profit is a religious organization, employees are expected, even if the Not-For-Profit does not pay the Social Security, to pay it through their paycheck as if they are self-employed.

But it turns out that this is still a confused area, as some internet sites still claim that Not-For-Profits are not required to pay Social Security, others say the employee is on the hook, and still others say that most Not-For-Profits pay it voluntarily. I once worked for a non-religious Not-For-Profit where I was told, after I was hired, that they did **not** pay into SS and I was glad that I moved on; they, however, had some employees who had been there as long as a decade.

Regardless of the black and white legality of it, what it means is that if someone worked for the kind of

Not-For-Profit that did *not* pay Social Security, or *did not properly deduct it* from paychecks for many years, <u>and</u> there was no retirement plan, perhaps the rest of us will have to pick up this person's complete tab at some point. Religious nonprofits are totally exempt and we have a lot of people working for them.

This future exposure is an *off the books* and yet to be calculated obligation of this country should the person have no savings. I am thinking maybe somebody should figure out how to add it to the other obligations so we know what our REAL expected financial risks are for this blunder. I suspect it is much larger than people think it could be.

Now the argument for having social service Not-For-Profits has been that they can do things more *cheaply* than the government could or would locally. That is probably true, (*especially if they are not paying into Social Security)*, but then I believe we have the right to demand that they are run competently if their role is to replace government.

My question: *Do you think that we should have some law to ensure that those who do not pay into Social Security are required to offer something equivalent to their employees?*

You decide.

If I were one of Gate-Buffet's Executive Philanthropists, I would make sure organizations were paying Social Security. You'd think that would not be hard, but I ask:

Just who, Mr. or Ms. Executive Philanthropist, are you giving your dollars to?

I hate to say it, because I really am a centrist, but because I have been there and seen that, I believe there really is a Left-leaning group who intentionally launch nonprofits using the government, foundations and individual donors to fund very comfortable personal lifestyles while they do nothing economically to add new dollars to our economy.

I hate to say it because I don't say this to cause political polarization, but it's really just too big an issue to ignore, and so I take the chance that my comments will be distorted. I say it to surface this information into the conscious conversation I feel we Americans need to have to avoid falling over the edge of the cliff and meeting Rome on the bottom. I say it because there are signs that we intend to entrust more health care work to some of these often undertrained and often *very* manipulative people.

It's hard for me to hide some bias against this cohort, for when considered together, I believe they are the most incompetent managers I have ever encountered.

But to be clear, my critique of them is about their managerial skillsets and my observations of voids in character. It is not personal. I actually have liked a lot of them: they are often witty, for instance. And if they were Right leaning and had the same skill set when considered as a group, I'd have the same dang opinion.

So my questions become:

- *What's the difference between the traditional Left seeking class parity through increased taxes and Executive Philanthropists giving money to Not-For-Profits?*

- *Has the Left in fact **manipulated** Executive Philanthropists into taking on the Left's traditional role?*

- *In other words, is the Philanthropic Right now the New Left?*

You decide.

What I will say, as we move on here, is that it's not only factors of undertraining, the motive to avoid hard work, or what the historical comparative per-spective about philanthropy is that merge together here to create the morass that I am about to take this discussion deep into.

The fact is, the work interface just gets far more complicated when badly written or interpreted laws are brought into the conversation - - and so we go...

THE AMERICANS WITH DISABILITIES ACT

Now this is where a little reminder might do some good: again, some of the comments I make here are dramatized and/or fictionalized from various stories presented to me as "the truth somewhere in America".

I think most of us would agree that complicating work life are laws and the lawyers who make a good living making new laws and interpreting existing laws. I will add that things have become very complicated in how organizations respond to dysfunction, particularly when it involves *the ADA law.*

For some backstory, the Americans with Disability Act (ADA) is a Federal law that was passed in 1990 to prevent discrimination against those with disabilities. In my view, the ADA law is great for the physically disabled in terms of what their rights are at work.

The language about reasonable accommodations was nearly perfect for eliminating physical barriers that impeded their ability to take on positions for which they were otherwise intellectually, educationally, and emotionally qualified.

BUT - in my opinion, what this law has also done is create both a nightmare for employees and organizations, and become a boon for the legal industry due to the ADA's protection of those who assert mental illness.

I have some knowledge about mental illness, having employed a young man who had an imbalance in brain chemistry who took medication for it. He was fine in a basic maintenance position, but would I have hired him for a more skilled position? Heck no. Why? Because even though he was on medication, he was still too unstable to be put in charge of machinery or oversee other staff; in other words, he was appropriately employed.

It used to be that mentally unstable or ill people were *naturally* placed into jobs that they could actually accomplish. This was seen as their lot in life, nature decided it for them, and organizations were not expected to drain resources to allow them to keep positions they were not able to perform simply to avoid potential lawsuits.

Now, what's been happening widely, given my conversations with lawyers, academics, colleagues, and friends, is that some organizations seem to think they can't fire anyone who claims an ADA accommodation for mental illness, and so the water cooler talk these days is that managers feel their executives are being poorly advised by lawyers; and from what I have read on lawyer blogs in particular, the water cooler talk is likely correct.

It's my opinion, after much research, that at least some lawyers are improperly recommending the most cost efficient way of handling these situations is at the expense of some good people's legal right to *due process* and *whistleblower* protections. I've been told of at least three stories in recent years where employment lawyers advised executives to take path of exiting (usually quietly and with a payoff) a protected whistleblower than to rightfully and legally fire an incompetent staffer - someone who claimed ADA protection - even when there was little or no concrete evidence to show that they were mentally ill other than a doctor's note and the word of their supervisor who had documented the assertion.

The ADA law was touted as being there to protect job loss for the person who could use sick days to handle their depression, maybe take a couple of vacation days, get it under control and come back to work. I have no problem with *that* use of the law for mental illness, or for situations where medication is the difference for someone who actually can do what's required in a job. But I now believe, and the research of the psychologists I referred to earlier supports me, that *there are a good number of people out there who are* <u>*faking*</u> *it, partially or completely.*

I have been told of instances where half the office is informed that someone is mentally ill, the other half is not. Further, the claim has been made that the people who should know since their jobs are connected closely to a person *are not* told, and the ones that have no business knowing about it, *are* told. Since the ADA law allows for the person who asserting mentally illness to tell everyone that they are receiving accommodations and still keep their job, it's my opinion that in a small organization, *they should at least tell their peers*, if not everyone, for that would not only protect them more clearly, but it would give everyone the opportunity to learn about mental illness in an open way.

Since the ADA law protects the person if they self disclose, it would require everyone to keep it confidential subject to a *personal* lawsuit, for disclosure to external parties is seen as acting outside the scope of their duties. If that legal exposure is made clear to individuals, then everyone would know what they stood to lose if they improperly disclose the person's status.

And, as someone reminded me recently, *the best kept secret can be the one everyone knows*. I believe that for truly mentally ill staffers who can otherwise perform the duties of their job, people would rally for them if they knew, because if co-workers are not given this opportunity to rally for the person, then accusations of unfair treatment fly. I also believe with more self-disclosure of reasonable accommodations, fakers would be more easily flushed out.

In my opinion, this is now a *huge* but unsurfaced problem in this country, one that is affecting work life far more than the average employee has any idea about - *it's happening at a workplace near you* - but here we should start with a little context first.

THE MYTH OF FAIRNESS

I am going to wax a little poetically here.

So Americans are encouraged to dream big. As I think I have alluded to, we can become hero worshippers of our own legacies, paid for by our names on the wall of a building, made more so whenever we forget that our lives are small blips if seen against the great panorama of the Universe's infinite clock.

We make plans and goals; we start families and buy homes. We feel entitled to pursue happiness – after all, it was proclaimed as our right in the Declaration of Independence, and we have historically felt particularly assured of this future should we have done everything we were told would result in our success story.

Moreover, that one could simply bootstrap it up the social strata has been a uniquely American possibility as compared with other countries, but recent events in America have called the American Dream into question. And, for a long time in this country, the variation in lifestyles or in social strata perhaps were not significant enough or salient enough to create large forces seeking change, though that seems to be changing.

Further, while we as a nation find ourselves somewhat confused and clamoring for what we may have felt was our God-given and/or legal right to own and expand our wealth, now the entire world it seems to

be in competition for these American-driven experiences of middle class "home and hearth".

As a result, because I believe that the world's
demand for natural resources will reduce the avail-
ability of goods, an American Dream that includes
high consumption patterns for everyone is probably
not attainable, even if everyone everywhere were
simply satisfied with reaching the lifestyle level of
the American middle class. Still, people go to work
every day, bringing that ideal with them.

MANAGING AMERICAN WORKPLACES

The overarching challenge for those who manage
in America, particularly those who wish to manage
ethically, is complicated by the fact that employees
and other stakeholders bring agendas into the organization that impede the free and easy accomplishment of goals.

People expect their American Dream to be fulfilled
by employment, and so for many, having their goals
thwarted by employment experiences leaves them
frustrated, angry, and unresolved, perhaps even depressed and seeking pharmaceutical assistance.

Those who hold *good character* as a value may take
some of this frustration out in small ways – venting
to a co-worker about not getting a promotion or
pilfering a few pencils. However, some who feel that
employment should result in a level of "home and
hearth" as defined by Architectural Digest rationalize

a different approach to dealing with frustration and ensuring that their economic needs are met. In a nutshell, they play *dirty*.

Dr. George Simon, in the book, "*In Sheep's Clothing*" calls these people "covert-aggressors", or in other words, people who actively make work environments toxic for their co-workers because their only main and very vibrant goal is "*what's in it for me*?". Their behavior impedes the health of the organization itself, and when covert-aggressors have senior management or Board members on their side, their dysfunction, often measured in staff turnover, can go on for many years.

In the book "*Snakes in Suits: When Psychopaths go to Work*", authors Dr. Paul Babiak and Dr. Robert Hare come to the conclusion that some people simply are lacking in character to such an extent that *they consciously damage people <u>and</u> careers in justification for their own advancement*; unfortunately, they state that many of them do it because they enjoy it and would do it anyway just to make another person's life miserable.

To condense all three authors, and with a nod to Dr. Martha Stout, author of *The Sociopath Next Door*, my interpretation of their views is that there exists in our society a range of *character disordered personalities*, from mild to psychopathic, and that at the end of the scale, the psychopathic person simply does not care about anyone but themselves.

These psychologists state that studies show that the extreme, psychopathology, is a blend of biology and environment and that conduct disordered youth may only be *dissuadable* from adopting that life strategy.

Their point is that <u>it is a choice</u> these people make. It is not a biological imperative and it is **not** a chemical imbalance. In other words, **character disorder is not a mental illness or a disability that is protected by the ADA law.**

The key for healthy and well trained managers to understand is that people with *character disorders* may comprise *an impactful percentage* of their workers, that the behavior is potentially dissuadable, but probably not by them. It is important to understand that having even just **one** of them aboard immediately triggers significant litigation exposure.

Unless a critical mass of Americans realizes that accepting or ignoring voids in character is <u>not</u> working for us anymore, the odds are against those who hire such people. The newer behavioral inventories used in hiring these days are helping, according to the psychologists, but character disordered people often know how to get around them.

Character disordered people differ from what I have earlier called people with voids in character, but not by much, and sometimes, *not at all;* I believe it is a fine line sometimes, as do the psychologists. Those with small or intermittent voids in character are perhaps you, me, and the otherwise ethically motivated person, who may or may not be churchgoing, but who *course correct* if they do *a little bit of bad*. In other words, most people have a conscience.

To make it clearer, in my opinion, and with reference to the descriptions given by the doctors, *strongly character disordered* folks are like Ned and Terri in Chapter 3, while *clinical psychopaths* are like Betty of Betty's Lair who have no remorse such that their brains often do not register empathy. They caution against the reader diagnosing people as clinical psychopaths based on reading their books, and so I repeat that warning here, but I think you get the picture.

According to Dr. Hare, clinically diagnosable psychopaths comprise about 1% of the population, while Dr. Stout claims up to 4% are sociopaths. I think either number is far too high to be comfortable with. The number of character disordered people I believe, is probably as high as 20% of our population and growing, if my own experiences are any gauge. I would contend another 20%+ of our population is highly apathetic to character disordered behavior and look the other way if given a choice, and on that basis: the numbers are high, way too high.

You may think I am painting too broad a brush, but should you happen to read the books to which I have referred and find that you can relate to the examples here with ease then I would ask you to look hard at how you explained some behavior in your workplace. Maybe not everything that happened is what you thought happened or were told happened.

In sum, it's my opinion that over the past several decades, a lot of pretty messed up folks have figured out how to thrive in our work places at the expense of others.

As a point of comparison, assertive people make headway in a healthy arena of competition on a fair playing field and exhibit excellence; *covert-aggressive* and *character disordered* people try to change the field or play dirty to get theirs; most of them do this at levels of stealth and so it can be hard to catch them in the act, and often not before they cause serious damage to the career of others.

THE TICK TOCK OF COMPANIES

External competition is generally sufficient motivation for the average entity to find sufficient challenge to reach goals, but corporations need people in order to operate and sometimes those people do not get along.

In the spectrum of conflict at work, on the low end, we have simple misunderstandings, then minor internal politics or people just not liking someone's style. If we move along the spectrum, we find people behaving without consideration for others (perhaps including some of the ~20% who are on medication); then we see passive aggressive sabotage through inaction, then covert-aggression and people with character disorders and then clinical psychopaths, who spend every waking moment calculating how they can sabotage someone's career, just for kicks.

Developing a positive work environment is hard to do consistently, even without the character disordered. As a manager, you find yourself in constant flux to:

- meet the organization's economic goals and objectives

- make decisions within ethical expectations

- fairly distribute financial rewards

- ensure that employment rights are distributed equally and legally

Core to these efforts is an expectation that work if done properly, will result in personal gain, taught to us in school as the "Protestant Work Ethic". For some, this belief system drove the push to capitalism (Weber) and landed on American shores with the Puritans: *to each his own, by his own hand*, fairly played out (at least for white Christian males).

As we work in the 21st century, we may struggle to see the world as outlined by the Protestant Work ethic and the Declaration of Independence: *"... that all men are created equal, that they are endowed by their Creator with certain unalienable Rights, that among these are Life, Liberty and the pursuit of Happiness."*

The *created equal* part is probably what most people feel a bond with, and at least most people consider themselves to have *equal rights under the law.* As the average American grows up, s/he is expected to learn that equal does not mean equal material possessions; it simply means, or is supposed to mean, that when faced with legal issues, that s/he is afforded equal protections under the Constitution.

It does not always play out fairly, I think most people know that, and many find it frustrating. For instance, some recent DNA tests have cleared wrongfully convicted people, often those of color. It is not a perfect equal protection, but in general, I believe we are striving in the right direction on those issues.

Yet even with those exceptions, people still have the expectation that <u>at work</u> there is *legal fairness*, and whenever that inherent expectation of fairness is violated, I contend there is a deep loss of trust in the American Dream itself: **I believe it is deeply wounded if the violation of legal fairness happens in work environments**, not only for the person it happens to, but for those who watch from the side-lines silently, as a whirlpool of hope is sucked into a cesspool of illegal behavior and often, its cover up.

I also believe that not only is there a social concern with the exalting of greed, as in *Wall Street* the movie, but *the problem* with a broad acceptance of people acting without an ethical compass is that it <u>feeds</u> the rationalization of those with even *larger* deficits in character.

It is a slippery slope, or if you like metaphors: the ignoring or acceptance of bad behavior ratchets up the bar for those who act badly, and gives them permission to act even "badder".

Perhaps in contrast with your preconceived notions, MBAs are not trained to ignore the laws of our country. The aberrant behaviors you have seen portrayed in the news and in films are largely I believe due to people with character disorders, and never did I hear **any** university professor, or my classmates, suggest that businesses do not expect to compete on a *law abiding and legally fair* playing field.

Since graduating, it seems clear to me that the clean approach I was trained in, when it meets the path of action taken by people less educated in proper management, gets confused, mixed up, and abused when:

- Character disordered, "covert-aggressives", and/or psychopaths show up at work

- Some of lesser dysfunction but still carrying a "*what's in it for me?*" perspective people show up and align with the character disordered

- When the above types get together and *have a party* at the expense of others who showed up to get the work done.

Who knows why someone has a void in character such that they behave with excess aggression to obtain what they want from their work environment. Like the psychologists, I contend that it is *how* people are responded to when the crap hits the fan that impacts our feelings about what it means to be an employee in America, and perhaps also what it means to be a citizen.

It's my opinion that it is time that workplace dysfunction is discussed openly and honestly and is no longer shoved into the corner by calling these situations "isolated incidents", because they aren't.

Unfortunately, I believe they may be becoming the norm and I do not think this country will remain a country we recognize if we don't take the bull (or the character disordered bullies) by the horns.

To give it life, I came up with another fictionalized story to help open the dialogue about where we are going and what it will take us to get to a better place. I believe the story I present is happening in organizations *all across America*.

THE EXTREME CASE:

PSYCHOPATHS, THE ADA, & NOT-FOR-PROFITS

Just in case you think my bias about their leadership is driving the selection of Not-For-Profits organizations for this section, well you are maybe 5% correct, but the primary reason I am focusing on Not-For-Profits is that I believe they are the organizations that are most vulnerable to the situation I present.

As Drs. Babiak and Hare state, character disordered people identify and target certain types of organizations to "infiltrate"; I believe Not-For-Profits are uniquely susceptible to a more than average share of these people and I believe I can show why that is so. As such, I believe you will walk out on the other end of this story realizing that my decision to focus on them is in fact to help Not-For-Profit stakeholders become more aware of just what is going on so that conscious and informed change can occur.

As I have said, because we allow tax-exemption for these organizations, we have a right for financial accountability, we have a right to ask *how* they are run and, I would argue, we have an *obligation* to do both.

Again, I am generally <u>not</u> talking about the Kaisers and the Special Olympic type Not-For-Profits. The highly dysfunctional activities seem to happen mainly in small to mid-sized organizations, and sometimes government departments. Again, if we plan to ask Not-For-Profits to take on a larger role in health care delivery in the future, and I think we will, I believe it is vitally important that this vulnerability is openly addressed *now.*

REMINDER

To remind you, this is a story *fictionalized* from composite experiences from multiple stories I have read, been told of by others, and as well as a few ideas synthesized from my experiences; names have been altered and informational details have been modified. Just because I might infer that someone is a probable clinical psychopath or has a character disorder to dramatize the scenario, a lawyer would probably tell you that you should **not** go to work and call your co-worker a psychopath; you probably could get into trouble.

STUART'S REIGN

> *"Unsuccessful psychopaths are in prison.*
> *Successful ones are amongst us"*
>
> - a common contention in the
> psychopathy literature -

A Not-For-Profit program officer, Stuart, consistently waits until he is alone with his target to sexually assault a certain young man at the office. The gossip is active, but no one else has seen it to confirm it, and it seems bizarre because it is man-on-man, and so it has been dismissed as the gossip of a few disgruntled employees who dislike Stuart. Finally, one day, another program officer, Chris, sees Stuart assaulting the employee.

Chris was walking by Stuart's office and saw through the glass window that Stuart had his hands on the young man's buttocks and was squeezing them. Chris immediately re-directed and as such, Stuart did not see Chris. However under agency policy, Chris realizes he must report the observation to the CEO, who is a licensed psychologist. Chris writes up his observations and submits them within the 24 hour period required by the management handbook.

The CEO takes rapid action and meets with Chris, telling him that she appreciates that Chris followed the handbook and that the agency takes all such claims "*very seriously*". The CEO then meets with Stuart, and in response to the allegations, Stuart not only denies the accusation about what occurred but he takes the opportunity to gently remind the CEO that he is on medication for bipolar disorder and so he isn't able to have long meetings.

Just before he leaves the meeting, he tells the CEO that he has been having a bad reaction to his medication recently, and so mucks up the complaint by asserting protection under the ADA law. He then tells the CEO that he appreciates her support in helping him get past *this unfortunate but false accusation*.

So the next time they meet about it, Stuart acts insulted that it's still an issue, and not only does he threaten the CEO that he will sue and publicize the situation if he is let go, stating that he had informed the CEO about his "bipolar disorder" some years prior, but Stuart *then* demands that he receive even more "reasonable accommodations" in order to perform his job since he is now, due to this false and unproven accusation, further *stressed*.

To burnish his claims, Stuart gives her another note from his psychiatrist supporting his claim of being under higher than usual stress; the note suggests that if Stuart's duties are not further adjusted, he is likely to require hospitalization.

Instead of approaching the situation with business-like objectivity and an HR lens that would require a level of *legal fairness* towards all of the employees involved such that a fair investigation is done about what Chris reported seeing, the CEO instead feels compassion *for Stuart*, as she feels that it is only because Stuart is suffering from something outside his control that the situation allegedly occurred, and hey, perhaps Chris misinterpreted what he saw.

In sum, she has *cognitive dissonance* and rationalizes the dissonance away by denying the presence of other facts that might better explain the situation.

The CEO also feels guilty, as psychologists often do, as she thinks perhaps *she* should have done more to be preventative so *Stuart* was not put into that work relationship with the young man in the first place.

But if Stuart is typical of the strongly character disordered or psychopathic person, according to our psychologists' research, Stuart already does not do most of the tasks outlined in his job description; still the CEO had to fill up Stuart's time somehow and supervising the young man seemed safe at the time.

And since Stuart has asked for even more reasonable accommodations and has a new doctor's note, the CEO feels even more conflicted about it, but still she convinces herself that she has no alternative but to assign yet more of Stuart's job tasks to *Chris*, the witness, who has been railroaded for some time by the CEO into taking on Stuart's duties.

Chris, of course, has *not* been told that *reasonable accommodation* theory is why he is doing Stuart's duties, and it does annoy him, as it would annoy most of us, but the CEO *misinterprets the ADA law* and so does not tell Chris the truth. In reality, the ADA law does in fact allow for disclosure to a co-worker if the duties of one, in this case, Chris, are highly impacted by the completion of tasks assigned to the supposedly mentally ill person, Stuart.

Since Chris' ability to complete reports was dependent on Stuart's completion of work product, the ADA law *does* permit Chris to know that Stuart is receiving ADA accommodations; according to legal blogs, written by lawyers, it should be just that simple and Chris would then be advised not to tell anyone else.

What the ADA law does *not* allow is the information to be told to *everyone* unless Stuart does it himself, but since the CEO is a psychologist, she assumed incorrectly that the ADA confidentiality is the same type of blanket it is in psychotherapy.

However, as a result of her misinformed view, and even though Stuart has been reported for having committed a *real crime* by Chris (who himself lacks any complaints in his employment record), the CEO does not feel that she should put Stuart on administrative leave or notify any external authority other than the Board of Directors.

As a result, Stuart sits happily in his office, doing next to nothing, instant messaging his wife, and taking home a fully loaded salary + benefits of more than $100,000 per year.

According to the psychologists, character-disordered people are fully and consciously able to pull off this particular ruse, and choose to *infiltrate* specific types of organizations with these types of goals in mind. They suggest that someone like Stuart may go so far as to seek therapy and inpatient hospitalizations to effect the desired outcome.

But since Stuart threatened the CEO in the second meeting, she and Board of Directors are now afraid of being sued by Stuart and so, after a month of review, the CEO decides she should do what the Board recently recommended that she do: *get rid of Chris*.

HUH?!?!?

Even a few conscientious Board members asked that when they first discussed it. *Well*, smirks the attorney, *we have to protect Stuart so that the agency is saved from an ADA lawsuit of large proportions.*

But what's really going on?

Well, according to the legal blogs, the lawyer does not want any further witness observations of sexual assault to be made *by Chris*, since he already showed a willingness to file a written report, something that is able to be entered as evidence in a lawsuit, as in:

Didn't he know he was not supposed to follow the management handbook?

In my opinion, there are many levels at which the recommendation to terminate Chris is <u>illegal</u>, first with regard to Chris' rights under the *due process* clause of the Constitution of the United States of America, but also certainly if the handbook has language about whistleblower protection, and they almost all do, because it is supposed to be protected under our Federal laws.

Remember, Chris was not accused of *anything* yet the lawyer tells the Board that it is fine to treat Chris as if *he* is the criminal.

In other words, the agency lawyer's point of view is that since Chris shows a willingness to provide physical evidence that cannot easily be disputed, if the young man in question files a lawsuit, it's potentially going to be VERY expensive for the organization if the young man's lawyer finds out that Chris witnessed the abuse, since Chris is a credible witness. The faulty argument is that if Stuart then takes the stand in such a lawsuit and is forced to disclose his ADA status, then the organization supposedly has failed in its fiduciary duty to protect Stuart.

In my opinion, the Not-For-Profit lawyer thus *violates Chris's employment rights under the guise of doing what's best for his client by adhering to a self-serving interpretation of the ADA law.* If the lawyer has any cognitive dissonance to speak of, the situation is improperly rationalized that the organization cannot violate Stuart's rights under the ADA law subject to a lawsuit and large settlement and so, just about anything goes as far as Chris' rights are concerned.

They simply rationalize that it's just cheaper to get rid of Chris. But in my experienced and researched opinion, *the Board* does not really care about protecting Stuart's ADA rights either; in fact, many board members do not care about either employee's rights, as Ned showed in Chapter 3.

I contend, after much consideration of the data and the stories told to me, is that many Board of Directors' only real concern is losing their Not-For-Profit income stream due to bad publicity.

As the psychologists state, often someone like Stuart has done *this* calculus as well, and picked his employer carefully in advance.

And keeping it real, why would any psychopath want their supposed mental illness to hit the headlines through the threatened lawsuit Stuart said would be coming?

What naive Board members do not consider enough is that *it is an empty threat.* Stuart would not want any future employer to know that he has a mental illness diagnosis, because then he probably could not play his game again, and probably neither would someone who really has a mental disorder, so Stuart's threats of publicity are no real possibility.

They should follow normal HR protocols then, right?

But a good half dozen people have told me stories that suggest that *this cover up is the new normal*.

So why does it go down this way?

I believe that the empty threat of publicity is *the fiction* lawyers rely on in these situations; it pays their bills and they are perhaps seen as *doing the right thing*, especially to those on the Board who may also be character deficient.

As Dr. Simon contends, people who have aggressive character disordered tendencies often channel these aggressions into careers such as *law*, so it would be no surprise to me to learn that at least a few lawyers might obtain some enjoyment from ridding a place of a fellow like Chris and leaving in a fellow like Stuart, as Dr. Simon states that *sadism* is also a covert-aggressor trait. And I would say God help the person who is dealing with a Stuart, a CEO, a Board Chair, *and* a lawyer who are **all** character deficient or disordered.

So, after hearing from the lawyer, board members rationalize that getting rid of Stuart would clearly damage their funding and they begin to believe that they actually have a fiduciary obligation to get rid of *Chris*. It's their way to dissipate the cognitive dissonance that makes them feel oh so mentally uncomfortable.

And so they tell themselves something like, *"Well, let's all just vote together on this recommendation to the CEO and get it over with. My American Dream should not be thwarted by this little annoying event, now should it? Besides, the Chair said that it was just a disgruntled employee and that we should send a strong message to staff that they should not bother the CEO with trivial complaints."*

They have achieved what cognitive dissonance asks them to resolve: a place of no conflict and perhaps no guilt, and so they smile, shake hands, put their Board membership higher up on their resume and sleep at night: character deficiencies in full action.

As I said, from my research, this scenario is happening out there, far more often than you think. Often it is the grant contract or accounting staff who, because they are *rule driven* due to the nature of their work, will follow the language in the handbook and get shown the door. It's now my settled opinion that if you see a Not-For-Profit with a lot of turnover in the contract or accounting staff, take your money and run, because there are probably are one or more character disordered people in power.

Whether it is *power by position* or *power by ADA assertion*, in my opinion, it turns out that it is becoming the core of organizational power. From what I have been told, a lot of funding is being sucked out the door with exit agreements and attorney fees instead of using that money to pay for what you thought: saving orphaned pets, or whatnot.

INVESTIGATIONS

And what if the CEO had instead decided to secure an outside investigator to handle Stuart's harassment?

Well, it would probably go something like this:

What Drs. Babiak and Hare contend is that the character disordered person builds a team of coworker supporters *for the eventuality* that they are caught. What that means is bringing in an investigator could make it worse for *Chris*, not better.

The "Stuart-team", some of whom may also be character disordered, mentally ill, or just might be minor "*what's in it for me?*" folks tagging along for the ride, would simply tell any external investigator the lies Stuart has them believing.

So what happens?

As the psychologists' books relay, Chris' *allegations* are then turned around and questions are instead raised about *Chris'* motives. Along with Stuart, they claim that it is *Chris* who is not a being a team player and must be lying. Then the supporters likely tell the investigator that Chris was *out to get Stuart booted* from the agency from day one and that his real motive in bringing the now "trumped up" complaint was to get Stuart's job. For you see, there is clear evidence, isn't there, that Chris has already been taking over Stuart's job?

Probably no one tells the investigator that the CEO assigned the tasks to Stuart as part of "ADA reasonable accommodations", and instead they go on to imply that Chris is somehow unstable, perhaps even suggest that Chris is on drugs or drinks too much.

Open and shut case for investigator: *$ ka-ching $*

He likely does not investigate further than those the CEO suggested he talks to and even though he probably does ask for a witness list from Chris, he will likely have ignored that list, and written up the report.

As such, after consulting with the attorney, the Board lets the CEO know that they would have no problem with Chris being exited since the CEO should be able to trust her team, and clearly she cannot.

Note that the investigator probably gets a good piece of income from this attorney for handling investigations just like this one, so do you think he's not going to know the way the attorney wants it to go, which is, of course, in favor of the paycheck?

And in fact, one could argue that both the investigator and the attorney's incentives are aligned to let Stuart do his thing *again* to someone else, so it's not hard to see who it might *really be paying* to have Chris and others like him leave.

And thus *Chris* is targeted for organizational retaliation, *in clear violation of Federal whistleblower law*. After about 6 months, just long enough to let the wind die down, the CEO tells Chris that she is *not sure* she can trust him anymore because Chris clearly must have been fabricating the story he reported about Stuart.

While she says it more diffusely, she also admits to Chris that she went on a little witch hunt to collect data sufficient to boot Chris should she wish to.

Typically, someone like Chris gets the message and with negotiation, leaves the organization in disgust, is given some severance and signs a non-disclosure that effectively buries his story.

Further, the young man who was the target of Stuart's assault generally either quits or Stuart is removed from having contact with the employee, *just in case*. Stuart, of course, remains, and even if they want to get rid of him, the attorney may tell them to wait until there are enough other layoffs to hide it.

Now, if the organization had done just a little digging and asked for a second opinion, perhaps they would find that Stuart had duped his psychiatrist (and they almost always can, says Dr. Hare). Assuming he would even agree to it, they might find that a blood test shows little or no presence of the medication that was prescribed.

This is about the only way an organization like the one described here will get rid of a Stuart unless they become suspicious OR someone on board has been there before OR they read this book.

If they do not do any checking, they can be in a bind, because someone like Stuart is generally smart and has become an expert in what a mentally ill person acts like - so he knows when to act bipolar and off balance. According to our psychologists, it is quite the show, performed to psychopathic perfection.

And while Chris' career may be highly damaged by leaving without a good reason, almost no one cares.

APATHY

And so, in my opinion, due to situations like the story above, apathy in America is alive and thriving. I can think of no other situation that so well describes the character problems in America. At each level, people believe that they deserve their just reward at the expense of Chris, and they rationalize that Chris after all is well educated and will not suffer as much as Stuart had Stuart been exited, since Stuart is *supposedly* mentally ill.

The problem is: everything they did kept the poison in the organization, and almost everything they did violated criminal and employment laws, and *everything* they did told the other employees that supporting character deficit is *how* we run things here: *get used to it or leave*.

And most stay and keep their mouths shut should they see Stuart doing anything else since they saw what happened to Chris. And, in this economy, what choice do they have?

I believe these situations are now pervasive and pernicious in American organizations. I have seen several highly credentialed professionals become somewhat crippled in their career because they followed the employee handbook and were later exited for "*doing the right legal thing*". Add fraud to it, and a clinical psychopath can get off the hook for embezzlement as well, perhaps, as the psychologists say, even framing Chris for it.

Fortunately, the water cooler talk is that For-Profit corporations are far more likely to isolate the ADA-claimant and they are far more willing to exit people when they show an inability or unwillingness to do their job after "reasonable accommodations" have been provided.

Partly this is because, unlike Not-For-Profits, they are not often run by social workers who may make sappy excuses for bad behavior, but also it is also because their lawyers are not worried about a donor base being upset by a lawsuit. They would more likely call Stuart's bluff on the threat of publicity and he would be kicked to the curb.

But the problem we face as Americans is that now over 15% of our workforce works in places vulnerable to people like Stuart, and it's my opinion that these organizations are incentivized to hide real crimes so that their sources of income do not become aware of improprieties.

If Not-For-Profits gain more responsibilities to deal with health related services, and I think they will, at what risk are our parents and grandparents if we leave them under such care?

You want a little more support for my contention?

Just find yourself a CPA who works with Not-For-Profits and ask, off the record, how often they come across ineptitude, *generally speaking*, that is.

Also, it's worth saying: from what I have read, sometimes someone like Chris can look like they may have an axe to grind against the organization. They probably don't, but when the lies are tossed upon them, they are in shock, not understanding that *their* exit was even a possible outcome of following clear-cut rules and so they may react badly.

My suggestion is that should you find yourself in such a situation as a Board member, you should cut the witness some slack; they are highly stressed and they may be surrounded by very dysfunctional people colluding to keep things just the way they are, especially if Chris had to file a complaint against the most sacrosanct of roles: the CEO.

Right, the only situation I can imagine that would be worse than having a Stuart around, is that it's the CEO who is the character disordered person who is abusing staff.

And my view takes the psychologists' model one step further:

I believe that the American Dream is *the most accessible shared archetypal life goal* that is attached to by the character disordered to exploit co-workers.

In other words, if Stuart says something to his co-workers like "*they didn't give any of us a cost of living increase – who do they think they are?! We deserve more!*" In so saying, I believe Stuart uses appeals to the archetype to solidify his base.

And here's my inter-relation question:

Is what Stuart does to build his base that much different than the tactics used by political parties to emotionally manipulate voters?

You decide.

According to the psychologists, Stuart does this sort of manipulative appeal regularly to reinforce team support. Now strengthened by their experience in getting rid of Chris, the Stuart-team now knows that they can get rid of just about anyone. In other words, should no organization change occur in the interim, *Chris' replacement* is likely to be targeted next in Stuart's reign.

Note that if members of the Board were uncomfortable doing what they were being asked to do, they could have asked for a second legal opinion. You think any of this Board would have been willing to step out of the pack and ask for that?

Probably not; remember, for many, their motives for being there may be to bolster their resume. As I alluded to earlier, Not-For-Profit board members gain opportunities if they can leverage the role into a For-Profit Board that pays a salary; so bad publicity due to Chris or Stuart may not *pay.*

And so, for a significant minority of the board members whom I have known, their incentives seem to be aligned to hide anything that would get in the way of meeting their own "*what's in it for me?*" goals; the rest seem to tag along in apathy.

Here's something you might want to know: **In my opinion, secreting the nasty bits in agenda items that make it onto unanimously passed consent calendars, often following a closed session in a prior meeting, is just about their favorite *hide it* technique.**

Also, while Boards need to stay out of the day to day, they can *insist* that fair and appropriate policies for investigating complaints *always* be followed, and regularly change up the lawyers and/or investigators they use.

At minimum, *they owe it to the people who work there* and in exchange for the tax-exemption received.

IS THE ADA LAW WORKING?

Well, for the physically disabled I would say yes, the ADA law is probably working fine, but I contend the lawmakers never intended to allow character deficient and/or disordered people to manipulate the protections for the mentally ill to *illegally* influence decision-making in the way they appear to be doing.

My guess is that many of you were filled with *OMG* and *Aha* moments when you were reading this story.

So, here are my questions:

- *Which person have you been in this type of situation?*

- *It reeks of void of character, and yet perhaps some people would say that this is just every day life. Are you okay with that?*

- *Do you see how this sort of situation has implications for the future of America **if it becomes widely acceptable** that someone like Stuart can repeatedly get away with violating employee rights?*

- *Should the ADA law be changed or reinterpreted so that fairness and due process for all involved is front and center in the Boardroom in these matters?*

- *Would the ADA law need to be changed at all if the executives in Not-For-Profits were more fully trained in professional management, law, and human resources?*

- *Would Not-For-Profit Boards be run more correctly if their board members were paid?*

- *Is the prestige of having your name on an honor roll worth it if you know that there is a high likelihood that if someone were being harassed, that it would likely be hidden by the Board and its lawyers just so that **you** will give more next year?*

In my opinion, I think I have seen enough of this pattern in the sector to say that many Not-For-Profit executives now know **exactly** what can happen to people like Chris and yet, it still happens. What's nauseating is that it is done under the guise of keeping the organization viable in order to "*do good*".

So to potential donors and Executive Philanthropists, if you insist on giving Not-For-Profit careerists your wealth, I suggest that you do some due diligence. I suggest that you tell them that if you ever find out they do not deal with employee complaints legally, they will lose your support because *you* do not want that kind of publicity. Otherwise, in my opinion, a large minority of them are *gaming* the public to help pay off ongoing exit agreements and legal fees.

If nothing else, perhaps restrict your donations to non-employee costs and to non-legal fees.

Now maybe my idea that philanthropists re-hire their staff to do charity work is not such a bad one, huh?

A FINAL ODDBALL THOUGHT

So, though it might sound a little aside, I ask you to consider now that maybe there's another reason why the use of psychotropic medication has risen to 20% of the population.

Maybe instead of what you think it is, what you have witnessed at work is a bunch of character disordered folks realizing they can *game* employers into keeping *them* if they go on Prozac, using an ADA *you can't discriminate against me* ploy.

Not such a leap anymore to think that people will do this on purpose, is it, if it becomes better known to the public that an organization may predictably react in the way Stuart's boss did in our story?

Ahh, yes, Stuart's boss, certainly another character we should discuss: she and the possibly thousands like her can't escape a bit more pointed consideration.

THE LEADERSHIP DEFICIT
IN NOT-FOR-PROFITS

As you can probably surmise, I believe that Not-For-Profits Boards should try not to hire incompetent CEOs or Executive Directors in the first place. But, this is where this Joe reaches some subject fatigue, so this chapter will be short.

A friend of mine, Ray, tells the *fictionalized* story of being in interview **number #8** for a high level position at an organization that served ex-felons.

As background, the candidacy process had been absurd: Ray would have been reporting to the CEO, but instead of meeting the CEO in interview #2 or #3, which is standard to make sure there is a good personality fit, it was not until about interview #5 when the CEO sat down with him. The entire hiring process should not have taken more than about four interviews, but hey, *it's a Not-For-Profit.*

It happened that Ray had just left an organization where the policy was strictly enforced that no references were to be given other than period of employment, title, and salary. But as a courtesy and to be sure it would not pose a problem, Ray informed the Director of HR of the reference policy in interview #2; however, this information was not told to the CEO until *after* interview #8.

So, after two months of interviewing and 8 interviews later, thinking the reference situation was not a problem and feeling confident about his chances, the reference situation ended up being a deciding factor in Ray not being offered the position. The CEO was astonished that he would not be able to talk with Ray's prior supervisor and was upset, implying to Ray that it must mean something bad about Ray, when it did not.

First, it is now not uncommon to not be able to talk with a prior supervisor, even at C-level positions and it should now not surprise you to learn that Not-For-Profits who do not want their donor base to become aware of a lawsuit due to the mishandling of a reference check have strongly taken this stance.

So the CEO was uneducated about current reference checking norms, and was not informed by the HR Director about Ray's situation. Ray tells me that if he had known it was an issue after interview #2, he would have declined to interview further.

Ray also told me that they had been through two prior Directors within the past two years, and as result of this snafu, it became obvious that the Director of HR and the CEO did not communicate well or run things well, so he was in fact relieved by the outcome.

But that's not all of it. There was another reason Ray was relieved.

Now if you can talk like a visionary and you have a social service master's degree, it's possible to hood wink a Not-For-Profit Board, because they usually do not care much about what the CEO does as long as there are no lawsuits, as we saw in Stuart's Reign.

But this CEO did not even hoodwink: Ray tells the story that in interview #8 with the four Board members and the CEO, the CEO said that they were looking to hire someone very qualified like Ray, because Boards in nonprofits

> "*hire people like me who do not know what we are doing*".

Ray said his jaw just about dropped open, but a look around the table showed that the Board members knew the CEO was incompetent; one even seemed to shrug his shoulders.

This was another reason Ray eventually did not mind how it turned out, as he'd just left two incompetent CEOs in a row. As a result of this incident, Ray decided that he was done working for small Not-For-Profits and so we can see another unfortunate result: people like Ray who are highly competent refuse to work in the very organizations that might need them most due to these incompetent CEOs.

Ok, so guess how much this CEO makes? $75,000? $90,000? $110,000?

No, that self-proclaimed incompetent CEO was making about **$175,000** a year plus benefits; it is public information on their IRS form 990.

So why is that kind of person hired? Partly because a state may require a licensed social worker for positions involving certain types of care, but I bet part of the reason they keep him is that he *sounds* like, at least to the public, that he knows what he is doing.

Ray pointed me to Youtube interviews of the smooth-talking CEO talking about the 50+ year history of this agency and how many ex-felons they serve. In watching it, I could see how people could be fooled by the guy: he had it down, with all the heart-wrenching, donor soliciting tones a social worker could use.

But what the CEO does not tell the Youtube audience is that, according to someone else who worked there whom I ran into some time later, this CEO allow the cars of employees *to be vandalized* in the parking lot apparently because he feels that it would be emotionally harmful to the clients if security cameras were put up.

You decide.

Think the Board knows about this ongoing expense?

Doubt it.

A juicy place for someone like Stuart to infiltrate?

Absolutely.

Logical?   Not even close.

Typical?   In my opinion, yes.

My question:

*Think states should require these folks to take a core group of law and HR classes as part of being "**state qualified**"?*

As part of this research, I asked a university professor who specializes in nonprofit management about this type of situation and the response was that they know in the field that they have a

"*leadership deficit*".

Perhaps a leadership void, I thought, but I held my tongue and said, "*Ok, but Buffett and Gates are giving their fortunes away to these people.*"

He looked at me and said "*Yep - it's a problem*".

Which brings me back to asking the Executive Philanthropist, not to mention all the other donors out there, including you the reader:

Do you really want to have these kinds of people spending your money?

Again, do you realize that with that philanthropy, you are perhaps doing the re-distribution of wealth that you may have fought against for so long when the organized Left wanted you to do it through increased taxes?

Yeah, that's right, through philanthropy, in my opinion you may have effectively become a tool of the Lefty liberal, and guess what, most of the people who run Not-For-Profits, *they know it*, and guess what? I have seen them laugh at donors and taxpayers, all the way to their 403(b), 457, 401(a) and/or defined pension plans.

I admit that perhaps my statements here are slightly inflammatory, but in my settled opinion, it's now nearly a con game in some of these organizations.

So, do we need Not-For-Profits?

Well, probably, but I suggest that we should become more careful about which organizations we allow to receive tax-free status.

There is something called "*fiscal sponsorship*" that could be used <u>indefinitely</u> to help assure that more proper management and Board Governance is going on in organizations that do not need to grow to fulfill their stated mission.

And maybe we should let bad ones fail like they would in the For-Profit sector, or merge them with larger organizations where employment laws are more likely to be complied with.

I believe taxpayer and donor money is being used to avoid or settle lawsuits that would likely never even reach fruition were **good** Board of Director practices in place and were the CEOs **better trained** in good and legal management practices.

Certainly, no one can argue that Ray's potential CEO *should* pay for repairing car vandalism with taxpayer funds, but apparently that's exactly what he could have been doing.

So, you still feel good about these places?

Again, it's not all of them, but I contend that it's way too many of them. And, as of this writing, while I do not know exactly where or who they are, my research indicates that there are at least two organizations in my community where there is at least one person who is apparently just like Stuart, and there is someone else who is apparently just like his CEO; and the CEO where Ray interviewed? He's still there.

This dialogue carries some uncertainty about making blanket conclusions of course, but I can contend clearly that what we have going on now *is not working* and that we need to stop hiding these issues.

They are not isolated incidents and they need to be openly addressed, in my opinion, if we are to be able to trust the Nor-For-Profit sector to not spawn even more problems than the ones they are supposed to be fixing.

CONCLUSION

In covering a range of topics, I hope I have convinced you to take stock of how we have all, perhaps unwittingly, participated in creating a society that is increasingly susceptible both to dysfunctional ways of operating and to those interested in developing a world filled with havoc.

As I see it, we often now face, on a daily basis: mistrust, disrespect, irresponsibility, unfairness, apathy, and a lack of loyalty. In sum, the fabric holding together the American Dream has been seriously weakened and frayed by a lack of commitment to personal ethics. It is now systemic.

We need a society that more widely supports acts of good character if positive change is to happen.

People have to be able to believe their politicians are basically truthful, that the media isn't always angling to shareholders, that the banking system has sufficient controls to not allow the character deficient to take over, and that education has a payoff that cannot be destroyed by someone else's mockery of employment laws.

We also need to know that we put people in charge who have the correct training to run organizations and, lastly, that we do not let lawyers decide that an employee's legal rights can be completely sidelined - done under the false pretext of adhering to the ADA or another law - but in reality, done simply to avoid income loss for their clients and for themselves.

To close, I do believe we have time to change the flow of the river that looks to be dragging us over the cliff, but to do that, I believe it's time for us to *awaken* to another way of conducting our lives.

ABOUT THE AUTHOR

Joe Couch, MBA, is a former CEO and business owner. He took the risks and received many of the rewards of attending a top-ranked Ivy.

And like many others, Joe was thrown into an sea of unethical behavior and asked to look the other way. But Joe thinks that approach to life got America into a serious jam and that it is high time we had a more complete dialogue about America and its future.

Joe isn't much of a complainer, but as more and more people talked to him about their lives, they told stories of work and play that were beyond belief.

It was then that it sunk in:

America really is messed up.

Joe badly wants this situation to change, and he has a few ideas to share about how we can do that

. . . if we really want to.